A
CHANCE
TO
BE BORN

My American Dream

KC BERTLING

PAGE PUBLISHING, INC.
Conneaut Lake, PA

Published by Page Publishing 2021

All scriptures in this book are from the 1611 King James Version.

ISBN 978-1-6624-2390-1 (pbk)
ISBN 978-1-6624-2391-8 (digital)

Printed in the United States of America

Contents

WRITING THIS BOOK

Writing this book to tell stories of my American journey as the wife of an infantryman in the United States Army, with many exciting adventures, was a considerable challenge. For many years, I have written numerous commentary articles in the military newspapers, monthly presidential newsletters, and military memorandums, but this was different from any of my writings in the past. I gave many thoughts about which stories I wanted to share with the world about how it was then and how beautiful it is now.

And along the way, we have had many friends who stood by us during tough times in our lives. We have lost contact with many of them, but many are still socially connected with us. I pray that God will always bless them no matter where they may be. I also would like to give thanks to the many supporters who have encouraged me along the way.

Forever, I am most grateful for my privilege to live as a citizen of the free world, and I am proud to be able to say that I am an American. I owe God for everything.

I will be forever grateful to my husband, who has served as God's chosen vessel to be by my side all these years and has faithfully led us to be where we are today. And for our son, Sam Jr., who has grown up to become such a wonderful man, very carrying, thoughtful, and considerate of others. I pray day and night for God's protection and blessings for him.

I hope and pray every reader of this book will be encouraged by my stories and recognize God's amazing grace through his Son, Jesus Christ, my Lord and Savior. Thank you!

> The Lord make his face shine upon thee
> and be gracious unto thee: The Lord lift
> up his countenance upon thee, and give
> thee peace. (Numbers 6:25–27)

Many of the photographs in this book are over fifty years old. I apologize for their quality, but I felt that not using them at all would make this book much less than what it should be. Thank you for your understanding.

Pillars of Legacy Members

Hyosung USA, Inc.

Pillars of Legacy Members

Sam Bertling Jr.
Sam Bertling Sr.
Katie Blankenship

Brigadier General Robert
Drolet
U.S. Army Retired

Cherie Cain
Adelaide Cape
Edna Cole
Cindy Davis

Dr. Joe Fitzgerald
Civilian Aid to the Secretary of
the Army (N. AL)

Major Scott Gill
U.S. Army Retired

Sun Goodloe

Pillars of Legacy Members

Colonel Jeffrey &
Leanne Ogden
US Army, Retired

Marinita Haq
Stacey Harring
Jennifer Holliday
Helen James

Lieutenant Colonel
Ed Kennedy
US Army, Retired

Ana Lewis
Mike Logan
Beverly Lowe
Jill Mays
Brenda Miles

Pillars of Legacy Members

Lieutenant General
William & Marilyn Phillips
US Army, Retired

Lieutenant Colonel
Phil Patterson
US Army, Retired

Command Sergeant Major
John and Brenda Perry
US Army, Retired

Robert and Phillis Reid
Doris Delene Roberts

David Seay
Alabama State
President for AUSA

Larry Spring
Rhonda Sutton

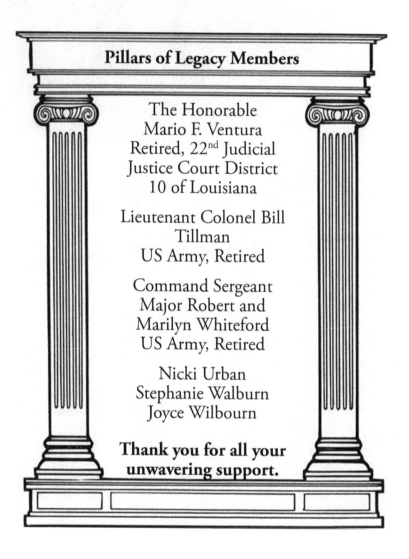

Pillars of Legacy Members

The Honorable
Mario F. Ventura
Retired, 22nd Judicial
Justice Court District
10 of Louisiana

Lieutenant Colonel Bill
Tillman
US Army, Retired

Command Sergeant
Major Robert and
Marilyn Whiteford
US Army, Retired

Nicki Urban
Stephanie Walburn
Joyce Wilbourn

**Thank you for all your
unwavering support.**

CHAPTER 1

A Cold Winter Night

Thus saith the LORD, thy redeemer, and he that formed thee from the womb, I am the LORD that maketh all things; that stretcheth forth the heavens alone; that spreadeth abroad the earth by myself. (Isaiah 44:24)

Photo above: During my elementary school years, we lived in this house. It was a beautiful house overlooking the river that divided the city to a countryside across the rice field with two bedrooms and one entertaining room with a fairly large front porch with a large yard. I was born in a dirt brick house with rice straw roof right below this house. At the time I took this picture, that house had been demolished.

When I was born on a bitterly cold winter evening of December (it was already January in the Gregorian calendar), the United States president was Harry S. Truman (Democratic Party), and many challenges were ahead of me. After my mother served dinner to my family, she then delivered me.

A baby girl who will grow up to become a dreamer, as she will be waiting for her prince to come riding on a white horse with a great ambition to have a better life.

As the youngest member of the family who didn't have much in those days, I heard many stories about how it was before my birth into this poor family called Hwang.

Photo above: Me with my mother. I believe it was 1959 while protests were going on in South Korea against Koreans/Japanese who were being sent to North Korea. In the picture, I am wearing a dress that was borrowed to take this photo. It was to be sent to my parents' oldest son, who was in Japan at that time. When he was taken by Japanese soldiers, I was not born yet.

As I grew older, I put all the stories behind me and wished for a better life. I don't have any memories of a happy childhood. I remember mostly being unhappy and having to work for my textbooks from the time I was in the fourth grade. I did so by cleaning houses and drawing water from the well for other people.

I rebelled against authority (except against my teachers at school) and caused many heartaches for my mother as I was a miserable girl who hated life. I cried all the time on the way to school with no reason, and I would stop at the gate before going into the schoolyard to the classroom.

Photo above: Me on the village mountain overlooking the city divided by a river, where other students were having a field day lunch. I skipped school that day because we didn't have any food to pack for my lunch. I can't remember who took this picture, but later it was given to me.

For the life of me, I don't know why I cried all the time on the way to school or when I was at home alone. All I can remember about my childhood is that I was very unhappy.

My teenage years were the most difficult, especially after the passing of my father. He was very ill during the last six months of his life with us, and I had to care for him when no one else was home. It was very heartbreaking as I watched him withering away from life.

We didn't have the money to take him to see a modern medicine doctor, and I was very depressed because of my inability to help him. When we were finally able to have a doctor see my father, he gave us some antibiotics to cure his coughing. But it was too late, and the medicine didn't work. I was devastated when he passed away.

I still remember the first and fifteenth of every month (in the Chinese calendar). We would set up a bowl of rice and some side dishes made of veggies on his memorial table, where we would bow and lament our sorrows. This went on for three years of the mourning period.

It was customary in my country to offer food for a dead family member and pay respects by mourning twice each month, in the morning and in the evening.

Photo above: This photo is the village where I grew up during my teenage years after my oldest brother got married and brought his bride to this home, which he built with my father. You can see that when I took this picture in 1986, behind the house is sesame seed plants not yet ready to be harvested.

During this time, I would cry and pour out my heart. My tears were bitter while I was thinking about how I wished I could have done more for my father. But what could I have done more?

Love for our parents was expressed by displaying great respect and obedience to their disciplines. I never told my father that I loved him, nor did he ever tell me that he loved me, but I know he did because of his actions. I remember at least one occasion, which I will share later in another chapter.

My life was changed dramatically after his death and as I grew older. Although there were no girls of my age in the village, there were three boys that were born on the same year as me. As we all grew older, I was not allowed to play with them, and we rarely talked to each other. Sometimes I saw them at the well, where we drew water twice a day, but we never spoke much.

I was under pressure to learn how to become a submissive young girl for whomever I would marry one day by learning to cook and sew. However, cooking and sewing were never in my vocabulary, nor did I ever think those were important to me. I was more interested in reading all the history books and current events that I could find.

While my family was waiting to find a suitable man for my older sister, I was not in much pressure to marry. It is our custom that a younger sister can marry before her older brother(s), but a younger sister cannot marry before her older sister. This rule or tradition was a saving grace for me.

While my life's dramas went on, I went to work for a wealthy family to learn machine knitting to make sweaters and other attires made of yarn, which were very popular in those days. The agreement was for me to work for one meal a day with no pay, but they agreed to teach me how to operate the knitting machine and learn the skills while I helped them. Every day, I worked very hard. Sometimes it was vigorous work, especially in the fall when the family was getting ready for winter weather. But I was far from being taught how to operate a knitting machine. I learned by watching and listening to the conversation and made mental notes to myself.

Later, I was able to produce some fantastic designs and surprised everyone. The family business grew fast, and they had to hire two other girls with their knitting machines, and they all received a commission. I also was promised to get pay but sadly never got any. It was very heartbreaking to see a family with plenty of money and food who did not keep their promises. I was heartbroken and felt betrayed because I had worked so hard. I decided to leave them and stay at home and teach village women and children how to read and write as a volunteer teacher.

During this time, I became the only letter writer for the village people who couldn't read or write. This opportunity allowed me to gain much respect from people and extra special food from them. Even though it appeared to people that I was okay, my misery was getting worse and worse as I grew older.

It seemed there was no purpose in life other than getting married, having children, and caring for a husband (whomever that may be). And if you happened to marry the first son of the family, taking care of his parents and his younger siblings was life's destiny. I wasn't ready for it, nor would I ever be prepared for this kind of life.

I wanted to have my way at whatever life might bring. I wanted to find my destiny. Sometimes I would have severe anxiety thinking about how my older sister might get married soon, and then it would be my turn. I had no intention of getting married through a match made by somebody else. But what could I do should that happen?

My family and the village matchmaking people worked hard to find a man for my sister, but she wasn't interested in getting married either. As time went on, I had the opportunity to learn English and asked other students who were in senior high school to help me learn. To this day, I don't know why I was so intrigued by learning English instead of Chinese writings. I was best in my class for English, but that was about it.

Learning to write Chinese letters was much more complicated than English, but it helped me to be a very creative writer looking back. Not that learning English was easy without attending school, but for some reason, it was easy for me to read, write, and remember the meaning of each word. Later I was able to attend night school because of a babysitting job. That family promised to provide education for me for taking care of their two kids (a boy in kindergarten and a girl in the second grade). This family kept their promise by sending me to school, and I was good with their children. I helped them with homework and went on field trips with them, and I was their teacher at home.

They loved me, and I loved them. I didn't know it then, but now I know that all that I needed was provided for me, and God was with me all through the years while I was growing up.

Learning English helped me to think about what it would be like to live in America with everyone who speaks English (to my surprise, not everyone spoke English in the US). Being able to speak, read, and write English opened the doors for several opportunities later, which led me to meet the prince of my childhood dreams.

> But when it pleased God, who separated me from my mother's womb and called me by his grace. (Galatians 1:15)

CHAPTER 2

My Siblings

Lo, children are a heritage of the LORD:
and the fruit of the womb is His reward.
(Psalm 127:3)

To share about my siblings, I would like to go back to the somewhat earlier days of Korea. Korea's traditional name is Chosŏn Dynasty, also called Yi Dynasty.

The word *Chosŏn* literally means "morning fresh" or "fresh morning" and is also translated as "morning calm." The word *Chosŏn* originally meant the beginning of dawn, referring to the fact that Korea is the first place on the Asian continent to see the rising sun.

In the old days, Koreans who greeted the early morning under a mushroom-shaped roof made of rice straw and while a rooster crowed would appreciate the true beauty of the appropriate title, Chosŏn.

I remember when the rooster crowed as it was an alert for the housewives that the morning hour had come and they need rise up to prepare breakfast, and farmers should get up and do some work before breakfast.

Like many countries, Korea's history has its share of war stories of good and sad histories. After Japan and Korea made a protectorate treaty agreement in 1910, little by little, Korea was annexed by the Empire of Japan, including after years of war, intimidation, and political machinations.

Japanese people moved into Korea and ultimately seized the land and its people to be subject to Japanese authorities. Korea fell under the brutal and forceful rule of Japan for more than thirty-five years and seemingly lost all its freedom and identity, which once had richly marked over five hundred years of Yi's Dynasty (1392–1910).

To establish control over its new protectorate, the Empire of Japan waged an all-out war on Korean culture and forced all Koreans to speak Japanese only. Schools and universities forbade speaking Korean and emphasized manual labor and loyalty to the emperor. Public places adopted Japanese too, and an edict to make films in Japanese soon followed. It also became a crime to teach history from non-approved texts, and authorities burned over two hundred thousand Korean historical documents, essentially wiping out the historical memories of Korea.

Finally, on August 15, 1945, Korea was liberated and was given the freedom to rebuild and form a new government. However, our beloved Korea was divided into two Koreas. The division of Korea began in 1945 at the end of World War II.

At the end of the war, negotiations between the United States and the Soviet Union failed to lead to an independent and unified Korean state. The Soviet Union occupied the north of Korea, and the United States occupied the south, with the boundary between their zones being the

Thirty-Eighth Parallel, with Panmunjom separating the two Koreas.

In 1948, after both North and South had purged their dissidents, United Nations supervised elections held in the US-occupied south only. The American-backed Dr. Syngman Rhee (이승만) won the election to become the first president of the Republic of Korea, while the Soviet Union appointed Kim Il-sung as the leader of North Korea.

This led to the establishment of the Republic of Korea in the South, and promptly, North Korea established the Democratic People's Republic of Korea. The United States supported the South, and the Soviet Union supported the North. Even though both governments claimed sovereignty over the entire Korean peninsula, today, no one can deny the differences between the two Koreas in every possible way you could imagine. Economics, technology, academics, and sports are just a few to illustrate how South Korea stands on the world stage, while North Korea is struggling to feed its people.

The division of two Koreas brought devastating situations to Korean people whose families were living in the South and the North Korean Peninsula. Overnight, families were divided into two countries. Although Korea was freed from Japanese occupation, North Korea was under communist dictatorship by Kim Il-Sung, and South Korea has elected Dr. Syngman Rhee as president. Even after that, South Korea had much more hardship to endure.

Within five years after being liberated from Japanese ruling, Communist North Korea invaded South Korea at midnight on Sunday, June 25, 1950, attempting to unify the peninsula under its communist rule. Both Koreas fought vigorously as the United States and its allies backed South Korea, and the Soviet Union with China backed North Korea, claiming thousands of lives and thousands unaccounted for on both sides.

Sixteen nations assisted South Korea during the Korean War and lost thousands of lives. The heaviest casualties were from the United States of America.

If anyone would ask me about the War, I would say that war is ugly no matter how anyone looks at it. Nobody wins in war, as there will always be casualties on both sides, and it destroys the nation as we look back on the history of many wars. One side may win the war and lose the battle or win the battle but lose the war, and it is always certain that there will be countless lives lost.

The Korean War lasted until July 27, 1953, when the armistice was signed, and a cease-fire was established. To this day, the Korean Peninsula is divided into two Koreas. Thousands of Korean families have lost their loved ones and will never see them again, nor will they ever know what happened to them.

To finish the story about my siblings, let's go back to the Japanese occupation in the Korean Peninsula when it was a major stepping stone toward the Japanese occupation of Korea. At the Japan-Korea Treaty in 1910, the Korean Yi's Dynasty has declared a protectorate of Japan. The annexation of Korea by Japan was set up in the Japan-Korea Treaty in 1910, which was never actually signed by the Korean Regent of Go-jong, who was the king at that time. After the Japanese annexation of Korea in 1910, Korea's domestic resistance peaked in the March First Movement in 1919.

Merciless Japanese soldiers crushed Koreans who proclaimed independence for Korea on the streets, and many were shot to death on the spot. Many others were severely wounded, and the resistance movement leaders were forced to flee to China. The brutality of Japanese soldiers toward Koreans is very difficult to describe here.

On April 11, 1919, Korea's resistance movement leaders established a provisional government of the Republic of Korea in Shanghai. In 1945, it was dissolved as Korea was liberated. During the Japanese occupation in Korea, my father was a member of the resistance movement in the town where he lived. I learned that Japanese soldiers found out, and soldiers arrested him, and they kept him in prison for a short period.

During his prison time, he was tortured by Japanese soldiers and was severely wounded in his right arm. I remember seeing him always shaking his right arm, and he didn't have much strength on his right hand. After he returned home from prison, Japanese soldiers came and kidnapped two sons and a daughter from my parents' house, and they were never to see them again. This I learned later as I got older and learned about my father's two sons who would have been my oldest brothers and a daughter who would have been my oldest sister.

The oldest daughter was fifteen and the two boys were eleven and thirteen when Japanese soldiers kidnapped them. They were gone before WWII, and both my parents died without ever knowing what happened to their three precious children. I heard that my parents suspected their children were taken to Japan, and years later, it was confirmed when a letter came from Japan from number one son who survived during the WWII, the war against the United States and Japan.

In Korea (in Asia in general), the number one son is a family's treasure, and he is everything to his father as his father's pride and joy. I also heard that my father lost his will to live after losing his two sons and a daughter. He packed a few things and left his family's land by giving up everything that he had, and he moved to an unknown city called YeCheon-Up, Kyong-Buk Province, where he knew no one and became poor.

He managed to find a place to live with his two other young sons and a daughter, and then later, I was born. Therefore, my sister often called me a bad luck child to our family because when I was born, we were very poor. I mean we were poor beyond any Americans can imagine.

Before I go into talking about my siblings, I have to tell you another story about my parents' three children who were taken by the Japanese.

I was in the fourth grade in elementary school. One day, a letter was delivered to my father. It came from Japan, and it was all written in the Japanese language. The letter was sent to my father's old hometown address, where his three children lived before Japanese soldiers took them and sent them to Japan. The letter traveled for about three months from town to town by word of mouth of the whereabouts my father by people who knew him, and it helped that letter find its way to our house. It was a miracle, and that letter brought a new light to my father and mother's life.

I clearly remember that the letter said the younger son was on his way to visit his sister in Hiroshima but was killed when the United States dropped the nuclear bomb that caused the Japanese Emperor to surrender. After receiving the first letter, my father replied to him and told him that he had moved to a new city. I remember that my mother and I took a picture together in my borrowed dress. And my father took a picture of himself, and we sent pictures to him in reply telling how our family had moved on. Since he didn't know I was born when he left, I was the only one to be in the picture.

The second letter came with a picture of him with his wife and a son. I remember it was a very nice picture, and he was a very nice-looking man, just as his wife and son were very beautiful. The letter also stated that he was married to a Japanese woman who nursed him in a hospital when he was injured, and they had a son, and they were planning to return to Korea. This was incredible news to my family and the entire city and our village, and everyone who knew my father was so thrilled. Then the letters stopped, and there was no more news about when he would come to us.

Later, we heard about someone from the city who will be taking a business trip to Japan. We did everything we could to raise some money to give to this gentleman who offered to find my father's number one son with the address that was listed on the envelope. I was about eleven years old then, I believe. I drew water from a water well a mile away, and I delivered it to the house to house to Agricultural Senior high school teachers' residents to earn some money to help my family raise enough to pay this kind gentleman.

We borrowed some and earned some, and some people donated as we pushed very hard. We gave what we had saved to this gentleman along with an address, hoping for him to bring the great news. As time went on, we were all very anxious for this gentleman to return from his trip to Japan. One day, he finally returned and said there was no such person in Japan with that address.

This news was very devastating to my family, especially for my parents. After all these years, their lost number one son was coming home to see them, but he and his family are nowhere to be found. How can a family just disappear from the face of the earth? They have to be somewhere. We took this gentleman's word and trusted that he made an effort to look for them. I am not sure.

My father again lost his will to live, and a few years later, he fell very ill and passed away. My mother was by my father's side when he passed away. She said his last words were calling his two sons' names as he took his last breath. All through these years, whenever I think about my father calling his two sons' names on his last breath on earth, I cry. Yes, I cried. I cried night and day. Very bitter beyond anyone's imagination how a young girl would cry when her father passed away.

I wished I could walk the countryside road that my father and I walked all day many years ago when we went to get some apples for me. But that old, dusty road where we walked turned into the main highway. Now it is no longer safe to walk between the buses, trucks, and other automobiles. No one knew how brokenhearted I was.

I rebelled against anybody who tried to discipline me. I caused my mother to pass out many times because of my rebellious actions. When my other older brother came home, he would lecture me as my father did. I only listened while he was home.

As time went on, I learned that I must get a grip on my life, and I would need to calm down and be useful. I stayed home and helped the village people with reading and letter writing to their children and for other things. My sister-in-law taught me how to sew and do cross-stitching, which I found so amusing. What she taught me became very useful later in life after I got married.

As I started to teach village women and children how to read and write, beginning in the fall until spring each year, I found some meaning of life and lived with purpose. This was very helpful to me during that time because the village people respected me well, and they took good care of me. They would always bring special food just for me.

Then later, a wealthy family in our village sent their young son to college in Tokyo, Japan, and a few years later, he returned and helped his family's business. Everyone in the village went to him to write letters to their children and anything else they needed. I was a bit hurt, but he was way above my level of education, so there was not much I could do about it. I continued to teach women and children during the fall until spring because the daylight was shorter, and they had more time in the evenings to learn.

But what I didn't know was that soon everyone would return to me for reading and writing as it was before, saying that I was a much better writer than a highly educated, rich young man. All I did was read a letter from their loved ones, and then I would ask them what they wanted to say, and then I would write it down and read it back to them, and they loved it. I think it was the gift God gave me, even though I didn't know then, but now as I look back, God was there in every step of my journeys in life. It took me a very long time to understand that God sent his Son to die for my sins, and God was with me. He had to be my guide because of where I am today.

As time went on, my other older brother got married and built his own family, while my oldest brother's family kept growing with more children. My oldest brother had three sons and a daughter, and my other brother had four daughters and a son. Neither of my brothers ever went to school, and their wives had very little education. When my brothers and sister were of school age, my father refused to have his children learn Japanese. Speaking and learning the Korean language was forbidden during the Japanese occupation in Korea for thirty-five years. However, all of my two brothers' children went to college, except three who didn't want to go after they graduated from high school. Every one of their children is doing great and taking good care of their parents, as it is expected of them to do so. My sister got married but never had any children. She loves all her nieces and nephews and spoils them as her children. And as for my mother, she lived to be a day short of her ninety-second birthday. She passed away in 1996 while I was living in Germany. She had many years of a tough and challenging life, but she enjoyed her grandchildren, and they all loved her. I was told that my mother would spoil her nine grandchildren.

As for me, one day, I realized that I must tell my brothers and my mother how sorry I was for giving them so many headaches and heartaches when I was home with them. Yes, I went home and told my two brothers and their wives and my mother how sorry I was. I could not imagine how difficult it had been for them to raise me to become a proper young woman who would not disgrace our father's name. It was especially hard for my mother, who once had her own maid before my father gave up his family's land and moved to where he knew no one, and she later had to work for other people to raise her children. After I made my confession to them, I felt liberated from my heavy burden. My resentment for their discipline and my guilt for disobeying them all disappeared from my heart. I praised and gave thanks to God.

I returned to my hometown a few more times and led several women whom I used to teach how to read and write to accept Jesus Christ as their personal Lord and Savior, and several children did too, including my oldest brother and one of his sons. My last visit was in October 1992, and by then, my oldest brother and his family had moved from a village to a city apartment. I was very disappointed that he gave up the house that he built with my father for his bride. I do understand that the city apartment has modern systems such as indoor kitchen, bathrooms, and much more, but I didn't feel at all that I was in my hometown.

Though I think about them every day and night, I miss the mountains and valleys where I used to walk on that country road more than anything and anyone in my life. Since then, my second older brother had passed away in 2008. The rest of my siblings are still there, just living apart in different cities. Things have changed since my childhood days. My brothers and my sister all did well. They are rich in their hearts with many grandchildren. I am proud of my brothers and their children, especially for my nephews and nieces, who are taking good care of their parents and looking after my sister.

Photo above, from left to right: My father, my brother, his wife, and her father. Both fathers are wearing traditional hats. These hats are for older men who are married. Both the groom and the bride are wearing traditional headdresses and wedding attire. The background is a silk screen that is usually used to divide the room. The front of the photo shows wedding gifts. My oldest brother and his wife raised three sons and a daughter. Their oldest son retired from the armed forces. Their two sons both finished high school, and their daughter finished college. They are all well-respected in their communities.

Both fathers are wearing a traditional hat called a gat. A gat is a traditional Korean hat worn by men along with hanbok during the Chosŏn period during the19th century. It is made from horsehair with a bamboo frame and is partly transparent in black color. Most gats are cylindrical in shape with a wide brim on a bamboo frame. Only noble class men during the late nineteenth century could wear gats, which represented their social status.

Photo above: My second older brother's wedding with his bride and friends. I don't know who this little girl was. My father already passed away when he got married. My second older brother passed away in 2008 due to colon cancer. He and his wife raised four daughters and a son. Two of their daughters and their son all went to college, and two of the daughters finished high school. They are all married and well-respected in their communities.

Photo above: My older sister and her husband. He passed away in the late nineties. They never had children of their own, but they both loved my brothers' children. When my brothers' children were young and bringing good grades from school, my sister and her husband showered them with gifts.

This is my theory about my parents' number one son: During the early 1960s, thousands of school children and college students protested on the streets to keep Koreans who lived in Japan from being sent to North Korea. I remember this because I was part of that group marching against the Japanese government sending Koreans to North Korea instead of South. I don't think the Koreans living in Japan knew the difference between North and South Korea. Later we learned that many of those who went to North Korea were either killed or sent to hard labor camps. That could have been my parents' number one son and his family.

> Children's children are the crown of old
> men; and the glory of children are their
> fathers. (Proverbs 17:6)

CHAPTER 3

A Basketful of Apples

For the love of money is the root of all evil: which while some coveted after, they have erred from the faith, and pierced themselves through with many sorrows. (1 Timothy 6:10)

In our village where I grew up, we didn't have many fruit trees other than persimmon trees. A few rich families had several persimmons and chestnut trees, and they would not let anybody come near these trees. Some families had very mean and vicious dogs to guard their trees as well as their houses. As much as I loved fresh fruit, which I still do, I wished we had some fruit trees then.

In those days, fresh fruits and veggies in the winter were very expensive. Fruits are especially are hard to come by. We were able to have a few apples, pears or peaches, and dried persimmons only on special occasions. Korean pears are so sweet, juicy, and crispy. I loved peaches and apples, and it was very rare that we would get some, unless when it was a very special occasion such as Korean Harvest Thanksgiving Day or Memorial Day of loved ones who had passed away.

My father knew how much I loved apples, and one day, during his planned visit to one of his patients in an out-of-town village, he promised me that he would take me with him to visit our long-lost relatives who had a large apple and peach orchard. He told me that they would have plenty of apples, all that I can eat to my heart's content. I was so excited. Not only was I going to have all the apples I wanted to eat, but I was traveling with my father. Being the youngest in the family, I had a few more privileges than my older brothers and sister.

I believe I was about six or seven years old then. We didn't have bus fare, so I remember we hitchhiked to get to where we needed to go. Some kind and rich family with their private vehicle drove us to the nearest town to the village of my father's patient, and we walked the rest of the way. We spent a night there after seeing a young man who was recovering from his sickness, and the family treated us very kindly and kept thanking my father for his medicine that helped to cure their son's illness.

Finally, early the next day, we walked all day to our long-lost relative's house. In the village where we visited the sickly young man, there was no transportation, so we had to walk almost half of the country. When we finally reached our long-lost relative's house, we spent the night there.

I remember hearing my father telling them that he brought me with him to their house so I could have some apples to eat. After dinner, the family and their house workers gathered and sorted out apples for the market the next day. Later they brought a basketful of apples and told me to eat all I wanted but warned me if that I eat too many, I would have a belly ache later. And my father also reminded me not to eat too many but to save some for the next day.

To my surprise and disappointment for the rest of my life, the basketful of apples was all spoiled, and not even one apple could give me a bite to eat; instead, it would make me sick by just looking at them. I was so disappointed and hurt that with all those apples, not even one I could eat. I did not eat any of it. To this day, I am proud that I didn't eat any of their apples.

Later, when we went to bed (not an actual bed but on the floor with a blanket), my father asked me if I had enough apples to satisfy my heart. I cried and told him that I did not eat any, and I never want to come to their house again as long as I live. When he asked why, I told him that all the apples in the basket were spoiled and rotten. We never went back, and I have no idea what happened to them or if my father ever visited them again.

On our way home the next day, my father stopped at a small country store by the roadside and exchanged some grain he received from the sickly young man's parents for his medicine, which was in exchange for his service. He exchanged a little portion of grain with the store owner for some food for us to eat on the way home and a few apples. The apples were so good, sweet, and crispy. I have never forgotten how good those apples were. My father was very pleased that I was not crying anymore, and we both had something to eat and enjoyed those apples.

It was a long day of walking and hitchhiking to get home before it was too late. My father carried me on his back atop of his grain sack when I was too tired to walk, and sometimes we would get on a cow wagon for a few miles, and then we again walked all day.

That day, my father taught me many things about life and money. He said that I was maybe too young to understand, but as he said that, he hopes that I will remember when I grow older. He said that I was never to chase money because money is the root of many evils. He said the money had to follow me. Therefore, I must never chase money. For the life of me, I could not understand how I have two legs but must not chase money, but money will come to me without two legs.

He said chasing money will bring many sorrows and heartaches because if I was never meant to be rich, money would never come into my hands and stay. Even if it does, it will go away quickly, and life would be exceedingly miserable and empty again because I will always be chasing the money. This advice never sunk into my head until later in life. Although I was never drawn so much toward money, I sure would like to have my share of it. Yes, I chased money, but as soon as I caught it, it would soon fly away from my hands. I was disappointed many times, but I finally understood what he meant that day.

He also told me that I was to be kind to people regardless of their financial status or their position. He said to me that I should always consider helping people who are less fortunate or who need my help even if I don't have much. I was to share what I can with poor people. I think he knew I was very selfish, and I wanted things to be my way. But what my father told me (to share what I can with poor people) always stuck in my head, and I wanted to do what he said to me because I wanted to please him, and also, I wanted him to be proud of me.

As a child, I didn't know we were poor, even though we did not have things other village people had. I never had new clothes and never had a new pair of shoes until I started school. Things I needed were always provided someway somehow. Even though it was not the best, what I needed was always there for me. And for him telling me to be kind to people that are poor, I remember seeing my parents living what my father was telling me. I remember that every morning when we had breakfast, my mother would always set aside a bowl of barley or whatever we were having for breakfast for a group of people who would come to our front gate and sing for a bowl of food.

This was very common in my childhood days after the Korean War. People without an arm or a leg or lepers would come to every house, and they would sing, and when they get some food, they will leave. They only came in the morning because Koreans usually eat a good breakfast, and dinner is usually very light with leftovers made into the soup to stretch for the entire family. We never asked why she was doing that and understood only that it was just customary for almost every family in the village to share their food with beggars.

Though it was a hard and very tiring trip as a child that day, my father taught me many valuable lessons about life, and to this day, I cherish my memories of that trip.

I never told my father that I loved him, nor did he ever tell me that he loved me. We display our love to our parents by being obedient to their teachings with respect, and we were never to disgrace our father's name. And the parents' way of showing their love for children was by strict discipline. We had never exchanged the word love, but I knew my father loved me. As a matter of fact, I thought my father was the only person in my family who loved me because he never laid his hand on me no matter how stubborn I was.

Many times, he lectured me about how disobeying the rules would bring shame to his name, and he asked me to be considerate. He made me want to obey his teachings, but whenever my older siblings spanked me when my father was not home, I would rebel more. For example, I was never to cross the street in front of an elderly man as he is walking. Rather, I must stop completely and bow to him, and then I was to cross the street from behind him.

Well, I didn't like that rule, especially when I was in a hurry. I would rarely look if anyone was coming before crossing the street. I would just cross the street first then see if anyone was coming, knowing that I might be in trouble. Yes, I got in trouble many times for my stubbornness and got more than my share of spankings. I hated with a passion, and I refused to give in to the rules that I disliked, and I thought they were wrong, just because I was a girl.

One other time, I had experienced how much my father loved me. He was gone a lot in my childhood days with his medicine bag to visit his patients. One day, I was very sick, but I went to school anyway. To my family, it was very important that I don't miss my school days. I was the first and only child in my family to attend school, and my parents were very proud that I was learning to read and write. However, my school years were cut short because my parents didn't have money, and since I was a girl and knew more than most of the girls in my village, they thought I had learned enough.

When I went to school that morning, my father wasn't home. After school was over, I walked with my classmates, and we crossed the bridge that divided the city and countryside roads. As I came to the end of the bridge, there my father stood waiting for me with a wool blanket that an American soldier gave to him during the Korean War. He was there to carry me on his back because my mother told him that I was sick and went to school.

He was proud that I wanted to learn and do good at school, but I was a below-average student. I think I was a very slow learner. I was good at reading and writing, but that was just about it. All the rest, it always took me a long time to understand the meaning of everything my teacher was teaching. My father carried me on his back all the way home. From my house to school, I believe it was at least five miles to walk one way, if not more. From the bridge to my house would be about three miles. Not sure of the exact distance, but I think no less than that. I always knew my father loved me, and he didn't have to tell me he loved me because his actions assured me that he did. Many times, I think about how deep down in my heart, I wish I could tell him how much I loved him, and I wanted to ask him to forgive me for the many rules I disobeyed, and I was worse after he passed away.

I remember that my father often talked to my mother at night while I pretended that I was sleeping about how concerned he was about me because of my stubbornness. My two older brothers and older sister were much older, so he figured that they would survive if anything happened to him, but because of me, being the youngest with a very strong will, he was always concerned about how I would survive, even though my oldest brother would be responsible for my well-being.

My father visited the Buddha's temple once a year in January shortly after Chinese New Year to worship and hear about his children's future from the monks. He would often tell my mother that I will be okay somehow. He said the monks told him that I will have a good life, though I may go through some tough times. I think it was my strong will that caused him to be so concerned. My father, even though he believed Buddha and worshipped the statue every January, would often tell us that the life of every human was in the hands of the sky God, and we must always respect the power of nature and look up to heaven for guidance of life.

From that long trip with my father, he gave me life lessons I learned at a very early age. I learned that being rich and having the power is prestigious, and it gives you privileges others can't get, but that does not make you happy. As a child, I couldn't figure out why I would not be happy with having new dresses and new shoes with plenty of good food to eat every day. I've seen rich families in my village and in the city who lived in a nice big house, but I had rarely experienced those people being nice to kitchen workers or anybody working in the fields.

I had also seen many families lose their sons or daughters because they were simply unhappy. My thoughts were if you're rich, you would always be happy because you have plenty to eat and nice clothes to wear, and you get to go to school and have lots of friends, and you would have a birthday party with all the village people every year. I thought that's what rich people did then.

I didn't know why many of them were so unhappy and even took their own lives, bringing sorrows to their parents.

Sometimes my mother would take me to a family where she would be working for them for special events, and I remember playing with the rich family's children. I've witnessed many times how people treated me differently when they found out that I was a child of a kitchen worker. To this day, I resent people who treat others based on their financial status or their position. I resent them with passion.

I have been very sensitive to people who clean the office where I used to work. I wanted them to know that they are God's children and that God loves them. I made sure I would have lunch with the cleaning team at least a few times a year, if not more, and sit with them and just talk and enjoy our fellowship. Everyone is equal in God's eyes, and we are all sinners saved by the grace of God through his only begotten Son, Jesus Christ, our Lord.

As I had experienced early in life, I am still experiencing today the status treatment in our society every day, especially as I am getting older, and when I walk into a store, most of the time, they would not greet me. If they do and ask me if I need any help and I don't reply fast, they just assume I don't speak English. It is very funny sometimes as I watch them and see how they act toward me, thinking that I don't speak English. As I look back that day with my father, I hope he is proud of me and smiles at me. Even though it took many years for me to understand what he meant about money and happiness, I now realize what he was telling me that day. I have come to where I now know at least a little about being kind to other people. I thank God every day.

> And be ye kind one to another, tender-hearted, forgiving one another, even as God for Christ's sake hath forgiven you. (Ephesians 4:32)

CHAPTER 4

A Beautiful Pink Dress
Came from America

> I will rejoice greatly in the LORD. My
> soul will exalt in my God; For He has
> clothed me with garments of salvation,
> He has wrapped me with a robe of righ-
> teousness, As a bridegroom decks himself
> with a garland, And as a bride adorns her-
> self with her jewels. (Isaiah 61:10)

When I was about six or seven years old, my mother and
I went to a city missionary Baptist church. They were giving out free clothes that came from America to people who
needed them. We were seated almost toward the back of
the church, waiting for clothes to pass down to us. As I was
anxiously waiting for people to turn down what they didn't
want, I saw a beautiful pink dress passing through their
hands. I was so excited and hoped that my mother would
accept that dress for me. Each family was allowed to take
one set of clothing such as trousers and a shirt or a dress.

When it came to my mother's hands, people around
us were telling her that it would fit me perfectly since I

was already wearing hand-me-downs. Perhaps I must have looked pretty shabby for people to encourage her to take that dress. My mother looked at it and looked at me, and then she handed it over to the next family behind us, and so it went on to other people's hands. At that very moment, I was devastated. I wanted that dress. It was the most beautiful thing I had ever laid my eyes on, but it went to another family. I cried loud and clear to let the world know that I wanted that dress, but it was too late. My mother picked up a shirt for my older brother.

Because I cried so much, people told my mother that the family who accepted the pink dress was one of the wealthy families in the city, so she went to their house and offered to work for them if they would let me have the pink dress, but they turned down her offer. My sister told me not to cry so much about that dress because mother was hurt too. I am sure my mother's heart was broken too because she had to get a shirt for my older brother since he didn't have decent clothes to wear.

Years later, my older brother, whom my mother had picked up a shirt for, bought a beautiful dress for me with lots of flowers on it, but it was not a pink dress because I told him I never wanted anything in pink, especially if it was a dress. He knew how much I cried for that used dress, which had come from America. I was so proud of the dress my brother bought for me that every night I would sleep with it. I didn't want to wear it because I didn't want it to get dirty. Soon I outgrew that dress and gave it to someone else in the village. Throughout my childhood, other than the dress my older brother bought for me, I never had new clothes, even during school years. And whenever I saw someone wearing a pink dress, it gave me such an empty feeling inside, and I've never wanted to see one or wear one. That was until later in my life.

In my heart that day, when I didn't get that pink dress, I had a dream that one day I would live in America. I thought since they had so many clothes that they could send some to Korea, I believed America would have anything and everything a child wants to have. I was correct. When I first came to the States, my in-laws took me to a grocery store. Every shelf was full of food, including pet foods of all types and brands, and fashions for women and men. There were so many clothes in every department store. It was so amazing to see how there was plenty of everything and anything. Nothing was lacking as far as my eyes can see.

I thought about America almost every day, hoping someday that I will have a chance to fly over there, where they would have plenty of milk and honey for the world and for me. When looking at a world map, it seemed so far, far away across the Pacific Ocean. But America was so close in my heart while I was dreaming what would it be like to be an American.

When I met Sam, in our conversations about how our lives would change after we were married, I told him about the pink dress. One day on our date, while we were walking around the city shopping center, he suggested that I should buy a new dress. My first thought was that I didn't want anything in pink until I saw one that was very pretty, even though it was a bit too short, but that was the fashion trend then. Nothing else caught my eyes, so I reluctantly bought that short pink dress, and I proudly wore it almost every day. I felt it looked great on me as it was the first time that

I wore a pink dress. Since then, I had a few more pink-colored dresses and shirts.

However, I was never a pink color fan because it always reminded me of that sad day, and I don't want to remember it again. But after wearing a pink dress, I was able to overcome the pink phobia, and I learned to live with gratitude for every little thing.

As life went on, I appreciated every little thing in life that I didn't have when I was a child. But most of all, I cherish the army family life and our freedom. We had no idea what we would have done if Sam was not in the army. We loved the army family life, though there were many challenges and separations during his active duty years.

I am so grateful for where we have been and where we are. I have more than my share of beautiful dresses in many different colors. No, I do not have a pink dress, but I do have a pink jacket, which my sister sent to me in 2007. I guess she still remembers how sad I was, and she thought of me and sent that jacket. I wore it a few times for her sake, but it just hung in my closet.

> Rather, clothe yourselves with the LORD Jesus Christ, and do not think about how to gratify the desires of the flesh. (Romans 13:14)

Photo above: After my husband heard about my pink-dress story, he bought this pink dress for me. It was a bit too short, but this was the trend that time. I loved wearing it.

CHAPTER 5

Coming to America

And the LORD, He it is that doth go before thee; he will be with thee, he will not fail thee, neither forsake thee: fear not, neither be dismayed. (Deuteronomy 31:8)

On the early evening of May 16, 1976, I began the journey to the United States of America, where I had always dreamed of becoming an American. Sam Jr. just had his second birthday in April, and we were to live with Sam's grandparents in Georgia until he finishes his remaining tour of duty in the Republic of Korea.

All my life, I dreamed of going to America, where the land flows with plenty of milk and honey. This dream of becoming an American was from my early childhood when my family, along with most of the village people, received used clothes and foods from a missionary church. We heard that all the goods had come from America. I too wanted to be an American and to become rich enough to share all kinds of goods with others who needed help.

Many thoughts were on my mind as I boarded the plane. While I was boarding the plane, my heart was beating as fast as it can. I thought about many things as my life will be changed, but to what extent and how, I had no idea. But one thing is for sure: I do not know anyone until my husband joins us after he finishes his tour of duty in the Republic of Korea.

I believed Americans were very rich and generous people and that the land would be filled with milk and honey and lots of pink dresses for girls. And they all went to church on Sundays or whenever the church doors were open.

My mind was traveling thousands of miles a minute, thinking about what it would be like living in the United States of America. Would America have streets made of gold since they were so rich? (Later, I learned that streets of gold are in heaven with a crystal river.) My heart was racing with many thoughts. Would there be any mountains and rivers like my hometown? Would everyone be as kind and friendly as I have always thought? I have always believed Americans were rich and the most generous people in the world, and I still believe that to this day.

My other thoughts were the following: Would my in-laws like me? Would I be able to please them, as I am a Korean woman who grew up with totally different traditions and customs? What if they don't like me? Would we live in a large house with many rooms? Would my husband be gone all the time? He was gone a lot for training and field exercises. Would we go to church on Sundays? How about going out for dinner? I wanted to be a good daughter-in-law and be a good granddaughter-in-law, even though I may not live with them. I wondered what kind of house the grandparents were living in.

I closed my eyes as the plane engines roared to take off. My mind was continuing in the fantasy land about how our lives would be changed forever when we all got back together and became an army family. One thing I was a bit concerned about was my inability to cook. I was never interested in learning to cook, so I was not very good at preparing any food. I must admit that I was one lousy cook. If a Korean wife can't cook rice, she has got to be in bad shape, and yes, I was. You will read more about my cooking in another chapter later.

As I was falling into my dream of American life, our plane took off with me not knowing when I would ever see my homeland again. All my dreams and worries, Sam Jr., and I fell asleep until we awoke while landing for our first stop in Honolulu, Hawaii. From there, I received a green card. I was told that it was a permanent resident card allowing me to live in the United States and that later I can apply for citizenship.

I felt so proud as I was overwhelmed and grateful. At last, I had obtained permission to live in the United States of America, and soon I could become an American. How exciting after all these years of my dreams!

Our next stops were Los Angeles, California, and then to Atlanta, Georgia. While flying from Los Angeles, California, our plane made several stops before Atlanta, Georgia. There was no direct flight from California to Georgia like nowadays. From Atlanta, Georgia, we rode on a big Greyhound bus all day to our destination in Winder, Georgia, where my husband's grandparents lived. We lived with Sam's grandparents until he came home in August, and we lived with them another month while Sam was on a thirty-day leave.

While living with my in-laws, I learned how to cook many southern foods such as biscuits, baked beans, potato salad, deviled eggs (until this day, I do not know why they called it deviled eggs), barbecue ribs, and other southern dishes by Grandmother Mary Bentley. For the life of me until this day, I cannot make biscuits like Grandmother did. Her biscuits were always so soft and fluffy, and she always made plenty for everyone to eat all day. No matter what I do or how I make the dough, my biscuits would always turn out to be hard as a rock.

Our lives began as an army family when Sam reported to his first duty station at Fort Gordon, Georgia, after his return to the States. While we were living with his grandparents, my mind traveled thousands of miles every day thinking about how our lives would be and what would I be doing as a mother and a soldier's wife. I did not want to be just a good wife. I wanted to be a great wife to my husband and a great mother to our son and to our future child.

During this time, I was about six months into my pregnancy, and I had very severe morning sickness at the beginning, but I was doing well, the doctor said during my monthly checkups. Little did anyone know something was to be very wrong. I was to lose this baby after a long six months into it. You will read about it in the next chapter.

Photo above: Me with Sam at the Sorak Mountain outside the 2nd Infantry Division in Korea.

As thou knowest not what is the way of the spirit, nor how the bones do grow in the womb of her that is with child: even so thou knowest not the works of God who maketh all. (Ecclesiastes 11:5)

CHAPTER 6

Once a Nagging and Crying Wife

> Blessed are the undefiled in the way, who
> walk in the law of the LORD. Blessed are
> they that keep his testimonies, and that
> seek him with the whole heart. (Psalm
> 119:1–2)

If anyone were to say that military life is unjust, unreasonable, unmerited, frustrating, and demanding, I would have to agree. Can we change the military systems? Perhaps not, but we can change our attitudes. To those who are going through tough times as a military family, whoever they may be, or to those who are not able to adapt to changes and don't see the need to make the best of military family life, there are many of us who do understand the challenges.

If you have school-age children, they may be missing many opportunities because you have to pull them out in the middle of the school year to follow your spouse's new duty station. Yes, it's not easy, and it is heartbreaking. You also have to leave the job that you love even though you might have an opportunity to be promoted soon. And many of us also understand how difficult it is to find a new sitter for your child(ren). I understand all that and more. Yes, I know how difficult and worrisome it is to send your husband off to a war not knowing when he will return or whether he would be safe wherever he may be.

I was like many who wanted things to be my way or no way. I understand the hardships you have to face and the need to make adjustments to pack and move on to the next duty station. Yes, not everyone is able to adapt to the military life so easily.

Photo above: Sam Jr. with Sam on his second birthday wearing the traditional Korean boy's birthday attire at our front flower garden in Korea.

As for me, I have learned that my life can be an adventure and an exciting journey. As we moved around the world to unfamiliar places, we've discovered there are adventures and excitement in unknown places. Many people must pay out of their own pockets to see the world, but we traveled for free, thanks to my husband's military career. Yes, we family members made sacrifices, but our sacrifices are small and partial compared to our spouses who serve in the Armed Forces. They are the ones who actually pay the price to defend our freedom.

No country on earth is like America, where you can trash talk about your governmental elected officials and still get to go home as a free citizen and then do that again the next day.

Here's what my journeys were like in the early days of my American military family life: It was May 1976. I was young, and I thought I knew everything and thought I was very smart. I must confess though, later in years, I recognized that I was very wrong. To my surprise, I was not smart at all.

Sam's first duty station since returning from the Republic of Korea was Fort Gordon, Georgia. We moved into a furnished trailer, and there were many challenges while I was recovering from surgery after losing a child in my sixth month of pregnancy. Sam was gone most of the time, attending field exercises or training, and when he wasn't gone, he was always late in coming home. I felt devastated at times as I had to cope with the loss of a baby, learn to adapt to American army family life, and meet total strangers. Perhaps my expectations were too high for this new life, and I was unhappy. I cried day and night and nagged the life out of my husband without a reason. To this day, I don't know how he put up with all my naggings.

Later, he became a drill sergeant. He did that for five years. One day, I thought to myself, this is it, and I've had enough. My life is not what I thought it would be as an American military spouse. One day, I waited and waited for him to come home. He called and said he'll be home in about thirty minutes. Thirty minutes passed four times and still no sign of him. I got so tired, angry, hungry, worried, and sick of waiting.

It was about midnight when he finally came home. As he walked into the kitchen through the garage door, I stood by the garbage can with his dinner in my hand. He walked in. "Well, my darling husband, you are finally home, and I bet you are hungry. If you are, here is your dinner, and you can get it yourself," I said, then I pitched his dinner into the garbage can. But he did not get mad. "Why don't you get some sleep and rest, and I'll fix something to eat," he said. Out of anger and guilt, I cried in the middle of the night, and the whole neighborhood could hear. I couldn't stop crying.

I didn't know how hard it would be to be married and be a good and submissive wife and a good mother. I thought when we came to the States that our lives would be rosy every day and that we were to live happily ever after, like that first kiss, riding into the sunrise avenue to the sunset boulevard as our hair turns gray.

I was thinking that once we moved to the States, we would settle in, and things would be changed for the better, and my husband will have a nine-to-five job Monday through Friday. I thought he would take us out to dinner every Friday, Saturday night to the movies, and Sunday morning to church.

Since I was a lousy cook, we went to McDonald's and Pizza Hut whenever we could afford to or when he got paid.

I couldn't even cook rice. If a Korean wife can't cook rice, she had to be in bad shape, and I was. My rice was always cooked in three stages: burned at the bottom, gooey in the middle, and raw on top. I felt so bad about feeding them badly cooked rice. For Sam Jr., I would mix badly cooked rice with some soy sauce, sesame oil, and some sugar, and I would tell him it is Korean chocolate rice. He loved it and said, "Mommy, I like your rice. It's crunchy like nuts." As for church on Sunday, I didn't know where to find the church doors. Movies? Can't remember going to any.

As my crying and nagging went on, one day, my husband sat down with me and began a family talk. "I can't be a good soldier if you are constantly crying and you are very insecure," he said and went on with more talking. "I need you to develop yourself and learn how to live when I am not here. I am a soldier. I serve my country, and that's who you are married to," he said. I paid attention and did as he asked me to do.

Now we've been married close to fifty years. Do you know anybody like me? If you do, remember there is hope for her. When we lived in Germany for almost thirteen years, I traveled to many military communities with speaking engagements, and sometimes he would go with me, and sometimes I would ride the train to the different military bases to speak to ladies' groups, which I still do.

Whatever I do, I see a sense of pride and joy in my husband's face as he watches his once-nagging and crying wife perform her volunteer duties and teach others how to overcome military family life challenges by sharing my life's journeys. I changed my views of American military life and found new desires in my heart many years ago. I learned that I cannot change everything to be my way, but I must adapt to changes and face challenges with a positive attitude.

However, we all know that just having a positive attitude does not make things better, but it is also our perspective in life. Through the years, I learned that life is not always rosy. If it is, we will learn nothing, and it would be boring, and we'll take it for granted. Life never gives triumphant victory without trials and tribulations. We don't wish to face the trials and tribulations for triumphant victory, but we must adapt to changes as an adventure. We must face them with determination to overcome with the best of our ability and with fervent prayers day and night. It is okay to cry out to God and ask for help because none of us can tackle our life's challenges alone.

I learned that happiness does not come to my doorstep on a silver platter. I have to make it. I thank God every day for every opportunity to serve in the community as a volunteer with my husband, whom I will always cherish for the work we do together.

I remember my younger days as I dreamed that a dashing young prince would come riding on a white horse to sweep me away from poverty, and together, we would ride down Sunrise Avenue after our first kiss to live happily ever after. We are now living on the Sunset Boulevard, cherishing our lives' memories and thanking God every day while enjoying our retirements.

It was a long journey, but it feels just like yesterday. Sometimes I would wonder how we became an army family and sorted through our difficulties in life to overcome many challenges.

Me in 1991.

Should we be given another life, would we live through the same lifestyle again? Yes, we would, absolutely and wholeheartedly, to serve our country together and proudly wave our flag, praising God for his unfailing love and mercy through his Son, Jesus Christ, our Lord.

> I will praise thee with uprightness of heart, when I shall have learned thy righteous judgments. I will keep thy statutes: O forsake me not utterly. (Psalm 119: 7–8)

CHAPTER 7

Army Family on the Move

> I will go before thee, and make the crooked places straight: I will break in pieces the gates of brass, and cut in sunder the bars of iron: And I will give thee the treasures of darkness, and hidden riches of secret places, that thou mayest know that I, the LORD, which call thee by thy name, am the God of Israel. (Isaiah 45:2–3)

Moving around as an army family to a new duty station, one would think that after a few moves, you become accustomed to it. It doesn't matter how many times you have moved; it is always very emotional. It was very heartbreaking, especially when we were moving to Germany. Sam Jr. joined the United States Navy for a Nuclear Power School program shortly after he graduated from high school, and the following December, my husband moved to Germany, and I was to follow him as soon as he signed for housing.

Soon after he left, I packed our household goods and left Fort Stewart, Georgia, in January 1993 to join him in Berlin, Germany. Our church pastor's wife and a best friend drove me to the Savannah Airport, and we said good-bye to each other. All three of us cried together. In every communities we lived, we made special memories, but Fort Stewart was very different for us. It was not that other communities where we lived were not special, but this was different, and here is why.

Photo above: Our first trip to a zoo in Seoul, Korea, as a family.

When we first moved to Fort Stewart, we joined a church started by a young couple named John and Tracy Baker in the Holiday Inn, where we also stayed until we could find housing. They named the church Grace Baptist Church, but it was just a name only. We held services in the hotel banquet room, and Wednesday evening Bible studies were held in houses of whoever would open their home to us.

Later, this young pastor resigned due to his wife's health, but a small number of church members, mostly military families, remained and looked for a new pastor for almost a year.

During that time, we had candidates from various Bible colleges who came and preached each Sunday. Finally, we were able to confirm a young youth pastor named William (Bill) Duttry with his wife, Pam, and two beautiful girls (Heather and Laura), as God had called him to be our new pastor. Dr. Bill Duttry now serves as the senior pastor of the First Baptist Church in Milford, Ohio.

Our church started to grow, and a few years later, we purchased a nice-sized property outside the city of Hinesville. We bought a used double-wide trailer and gutted out the inside and rebuilt it as a sanctuary. We also purchased a single-wide trailer for me to teach Sunday school class.

Photo above: From Fort Stewart right after Sunday morning church service at the Holiday Inn. We later built a very beautiful church outside Hinesville, Georgia, called Grace Baptist Church. Sam was the church's first ordained deacon.

During this time, Sam Jr. was homeschooled for almost three years from third grade to fifth grade. After Sam Jr. finished his fifth grade, he started the sixth grade in a Christian school about twenty-five miles one way from home. Several church families carpooled to help with time and gas expenses.

We decided to have Sam Jr. graduate from high school without taking him out of school again, so my husband voluntarily went to the 2nd Infantry Division in the Republic of Korea for a year-long unaccompanied hardship tour. Sam Jr. and I stayed at Fort Stewart housing until my husband returned from his tour of duty.

When my husband returned from Korea, our pastor ordained him to serve as the first deacon of our church. The communication between my husband and our pastor had gone on while he was in Korea, and when he returned, all went as planned. The church continued to grow, and step-by-step, we decided to build a church building.

Shortly after church members laid the foundation and started to work on the building, the Gulf War started, and practically all the men in our church were deployed. Only a few men who owned businesses were left home, along with a few elderly men and our pastor. All the rest were women and children.

Though things were not easy, God was in control to help us continue to worship and build the building for his glory. During that time, I prayed every day that God would help us finish building our church. I prayed that every nail that went into the building would represent a lost soul who will come to know Christ, our Savior.

Later, our church pastor's father-in-law, who had a large congregation in Ohio, sent eleven men to help our pastor to continue to build the church building. We all knew our pastor worked alone late hours for many days before these men came to help us to build.

Almost a year later, all the men were redeployed from the Gulf War, and later we had a grand opening of our brand-new church building with a nursery, baptismal pool, and brand-new pews. It was one of the most exciting times of our lives.

After returning from the Gulf War, my husband continued to serve as the only deacon of Grace Baptist Church, and I continued to teach children's Sunday school classes. Every Saturday, I went on visitation to visit children who attended my Sunday school class on a church bus ministry. I talked to their parents to encourage them to come to church. And every Tuesday morning, I would go out with two other ladies from our church to knock on doors to lead people to Christ, as we called it soul winning. I even wrote a Christmas play, and it was well-received by church families.

During this period, I also owned a flowers and gifts shop, and I made sure that every Sunday, we would have a fresh flower arrangement at the altar. I never missed a Sunday having flower arrangements. Later, I sold my shop to another military family member, and then she sold it to another military family member and so on for many years.

I am now leaving all that behind to move to another country. We had built a church. My husband was the first and the only deacon, and I watched my Sunday school class children grew mature in the Word of God as they move onto grades each year. Why can't we just stay in one place and live happily ever after? (At the time, I did not know God had tremendous plans for our lives in Germany.)

Grace Baptist Church Hinesville, GA

From Savannah, Georgia, to Atlanta, I think it was about a thirty-minute flight, and I cried all the way there as I sat by a window seat. As the plane pulled into the terminal, everyone was getting ready to get off to catch their connecting flights. A very kind gentleman who sat next to me helped me pull out my carry-on bag from overhead, and he asked me as I was still crying, "Do you know how to find the terminal to go back to your home country?" I looked straight at his face. "I am *not* [emphasis added] going to Korea. I am going to Germany to join my husband. He is stationed in Berlin, Germany." As I was saying that, his facial expression was as though he was asking me "Why are you crying so much if you are going to your husband?"

I found my way to the connecting flight with our shaggy dog named Doggie Sam, and about nine hours later, we landed in Berlin, Germany. And there was my husband, anxiously waiting for me. We settled into a newly renovated army apartment, fully furnished with all brand-new appliances, including dishes, flatware, cooking pots, etc. It was the first time we lived in an apartment. Everything we needed was issued by the government, and it was a very nice apartment.

Because the Berlin Brigade was closing down, we were allowed to purchase everything in the apartment, including furniture, kitchen appliances, and other household goods when we moved from Berlin, Germany. This was a great deal and exciting. I never shopped that much before.

A few days after I arrived, my husband went with his unit on a field exercise in Wildflecken, Germany, for two weeks. Here I am all alone in a foreign country again, this time with the addition of our shaggy dog.

I decided to adventure out and got on a bus, number 111, thinking the bus will bring me back to the other side later to come home. When the bus came to its terminal, a bus driver motioned me to get off the bus, saying he was finished. I got off the bus and looked for another bus number 111, but there was none. I decided to get on a different bus number, thinking I will find the same number bus down the road somewhere. To my surprise, this bus was going the opposite direction from where I just came from. I just sat there thinking he will go around the city and eventually he will go near where I needed to catch bus number 111. I was so wrong on this thinking. I came to another end of the bus route and was told to get off the bus again. I went to almost every bus in that terminal and asked them where I could find bus number 111, and no one could help.

At last, I found a driver who spoke English, and I told him I needed to find a bus number 111. He called another bus driver as he wrote down numbers and told him to help me to catch bus number 777. I assumed that's what he was telling him in German. I started to panic. I told him, "No, no. I need to catch bus number 111." "I am telling my friend to help you to catch bus 111," he said. "But you gave him the bus number 777," I said. Then he started to laugh and called other drivers about what I was saying, and they all laughed, but I was about to cry. I've been in Berlin, Germany, for only two days, and I am already lost, and maybe somebody is going to take this Korean woman to some unknown country. Then he said, "This is how we write number 1." It looks like 7, and he showed me how they write number 7. It took me all day to come back home to our apartment, where our shaggy dog was going nuts because he needed to go outside, and nobody was home.

When my husband returned from his two weeks of field exercise, it was time for me to get my US Army Europe (USAREUR) driver's license. Getting the driver's license was a bit complicated, and it was not about just passing a written test, although I failed at my first try.

They had me take the eye exam, and I failed. I was wondering how I could pass all the written tests and then fail on just reading the numbers and letters. They had me to read tiny, tiny letters and numbers. I asked them to make it a little larger because I couldn't read it. Well, the examiner said I will need to get glasses. I told him I don't need glasses because I can see fine and that he just needed to enlarge the letters. He was firm that I must wear glasses to pass the eye exam; otherwise, he would not issue me a driver's license. He said if I could bring a letter from an optometrist that shows I don't need glasses, then he would issue me a driver's license.

I went to an optometrist, and he examined my vision, and he also said I needed glasses. I told him that I don't need glasses. All I needed from him was a statement saying that I can drive. He chuckled a few seconds, and then he said, "Mrs. Bertling, I am sure you are a good driver, but you've got a lousy vision. Therefore, you'd need to wear glasses when you are driving." Yes, I wear my glasses now whenever I am driving. Those letters they wanted me to read were just too tiny.

As time went on, I joined the Army Community Service (ACS) as a volunteer to help them with office work, edit their memos, and do other small, not so exciting duties. I also joined the Berlin American Women's Club and served as their historian, and I joined the Family Readiness Group (FRG) and did whatever I could for my husband's unit family members to come together.

I also started to teach children's Sunday school at Victory Baptist Church, which had been started by an American missionary couple.

We went Polish pottery shopping at least once a month. Sometimes we would ride to the Polish border, cross the bridge on foot, ride a taxi to a large flea market, and ride back to the bridge in a taxi with all the cool stuff we bought. Then we would cross the bridge on foot, dragging everything we bought back to our bus in Germany waiting for us. This was routine for most family members who loved to go shopping. We all went out of the way to shop for more Polish potteries and crystals than we would ever use.

About buying stuff from Germany. We never had many collections at our house, other than just a few things I collected from here and there whenever we moved. Living in Germany gave me and all other military family members opportunities to acquire stuff we really didn't need, but we were buying things left and right with the little money I earned. My work was easy, and it was so much fun visiting Poland and Belgium for sightseeing and shopping during the weekends.

I did all this while I was volunteering at the ACS, serving as FRG leader, serving as a historian for Berlin American Women's club, and working part-time at the Army Exchange Military Clothing sales and later at the Quarter Masters Laundry Pickup point.

I continued to teach children's Sunday school class, and I did more shopping every Friday night around eleven o'clock at the Brandenburg Gate Market. Like everything in life, all good stuff must come to an end sooner or later; the end came too soon for the Berlin Brigade Army families.

Photo above: Moving to Hohenfels From Berlin, Germany, on August 15, 1994. On the morning of leaving Berlin, we are loading up more stuff I bought from Polish pottery shopping trips after our household goods were already packed and sent to Hohenfels.

We were in Berlin for only about eighteen months, when the brigade started to draw down and turned over everything to the German government. My husband received orders to move to Hohenfels, Germany, to finish up his remaining tour of duty. He bought an old beat-up BMW (mostly known as a hooptie) at a great price. We very much needed that second vehicle.

We packed our pickup truck with more stuff I bought after our household goods had been sent to a new housing in Hohenfels. We also packed our hooptie BMW with our shaggy dog (and more stuff), and we left for another adventure to a new army community. It took little more than about a half day to arrive at the new army base, and later we settled in government-leased housing in Velburg outside the army base. Our four-floor condo was very nice, and our dog usually got lost because we had never had a house that big.

I found another job as a recreation specialist to manage trips and tours and also implemented many family programs, including the Miss Hohenfels Pageant for nine- to twelfth-grade high school girls. This program was very successful, just as all other programs I've implemented. I went to Poland every month, escorting a bus full of Polish pottery-loving family members and had other trips to many European countries.

I continued to volunteer at the ACS whenever I could. I joined the Protestant Women of the Chapel (PWOC) and the Hohenfels Women's Club, and I taught children's Sunday school class. When I started to teach adults' Sunday school class, my husband served as the parish council president for the Protestant chapel.

Everything was going great. Our son, Sam Jr., had finished his Nuclear Power School and was now stationed in South Carolina. He had visited us several times, and he took trips with us throughout Europe.

Then one morning, I was driving to work and hit a patch of black ice, and my truck jumped over a ditch and landed on top of a hill. To this day, I don't know how my truck landed on a hill without hitting several trees in between. The impact of landing fractured three vertebrae, and I was in bad shape in just a split second. This was a very stressful time for my husband because he was getting ready to retire from active duty in the army. Since we had decided to stay in Germany, we had to move out of government housing and find a place to live while he was working on his résumé.

Helplessly, I lay in a German hospital with three fractured vertebrae in February 1996. Sam Jr. came from the States on emergency leave to stay with me. A renowned German neurosurgeon told us it would take several months before I could fully recover, if I would recover even.

All seemed dark, but God was with us. I was able to lead two elderly German ladies in my hospital room to accept Christ Jesus into their hearts with the little German I spoke.

Just twelve days later, I was discharged from the hospital and went to work within four weeks while recovering from back surgery. I worked laying on a long leather couch and handled travel requests from the Army National Guard and Army Reserve Units, who came to Hohenfels for their training. They would usually take trips during the last weekend before returning to the States. I ordered buses and coordinated tour guides in each city where the buses would take our guests for sightseeing while I was recovering.

To this day, I believe God was with me in that hospital to lead two elderly German women to accept Jesus into their hearts as personal Lord and Savior, and he took care of me to recover beyond anyone's expectations.

Later, after my husband retired from the army, we found a nice place to live near the base, and a year later, he joined the Department of the Army Civilian workforce.

He continued to serve as the president of the Parish Council at the Protestant Chapel, while I served as the president for the women's club and president of the PWOC. I was also taught the Army Family Team Building (AFTB) classes and assisted with the Army Family Action Plan

(AFAP) along with my full-time job. I don't know how I did all that, but I did. It was a fun time.

Then later, my husband received a new job offer to move to Wiesbaden, Germany, with a promotion to manage the welcome center. So after six years of living in Hohenfels/Bavaria, Germany, here we go again. We packed and moved to a new city.

After we lived in a hotel for a few months, we finally found a very nice house outside the city in a very nice small community called Niedernhausen Wildpark. As soon as we settled in, I went to volunteer at ACS again to manage the AFTB program. I volunteered for one full year for full-time and built a very successful team. We offered training every week and trained numerous new AFTB instructors.

After a year, I was asked to manage the AFTB program as a contractor. At first, I was reluctant to accept pay while all of my team were volunteers. Team advisors said I should take it. If I don't accept contract position, someone else might take the paying position and mess up what we had built as a team, so I did. My contract was only to manage AFTB, and with my volunteer team, we continued to provide training, and we developed teenage training modules while the program continued to grow.

Then there was a family member with two college degrees who joined our volunteer team. She was good and very hardworking, and she could have easily found a paying government job, I thought. When I suggested this to her, her answer was that she only wanted to manage the AFTB program, the position I was holding. She didn't want to apply for any other government jobs.

I thought about it a lot as my one-year contract was coming up for renewal. And I could have easily obtained another year's extension, so that made me think about it day and night and ask myself what I should do. With three months left to finish my one-year contract, I offered to subcontract my position to her if she would trust me that I would give her every cent that came into my bank account for the next three months.

Meanwhile, she could build a great relationship with the ACS officer to get to know her and take my place. There was no guarantee, but it was almost a sure thing. We agreed that she take my position as a subcontractor without signing any papers. She trusted me, and I kept my word. It was a bit hard, but I thought that was the best I could do for a volunteer member whose family needed that second income.

If I was in that position permanently, that would have been a different story, but I would have to renew my position every year, as the army approved funding. Yes, I felt I was making a huge mistake by giving up over three thousand dollars each month for the next three months, which comes to a total of almost ten thousand dollars. Nobody throws away money like that, and I must be a crazy person, I thought. I paid her all three months, and she kept the program as successful as it was when I left, and all the volunteers stayed with her.

Six months later, I received a government job offer to manage a community volunteer program at ACS. This time, it was a permanent position, and I went right back to ACS next to my old office. As I look back now, I still believe it was the right thing to do for a family member who needed a job and only wanted to manage the program I built with my team. Also, giving up that huge amount of money (about ten thousand dollars) afforded me to a dream job later that I never thought I would have. You often hear that no good deeds will go unnoticed, and so it was for me.

After a while, my husband applied for several jobs in the States, thinking it was time for us to return to the United States. He received a job offer from the US Army Space and Missile Defense Command / Army Forces Strategic Command as a program analyst with another promotion. So we packed everything and adventured to Redstone Arsenal, Alabama, and called it Sweet Home, Alabama.

I also received another job and hopped around a few organizations, and later I was hired by the same command to manage soldier and family programs. All the training I received when volunteering afforded me a dream job to work just down the hallway from my husband. Every morning as we walked into our offices, we were so amazed with how God had blessed us to be where we had come. All through the years, it was not easy, but we managed to make things work out for the best.

Who would have ever thought a poor little Korean girl waiting for her prince to come riding on a white horse as she cried all the time for no reason is now working in the same command with her husband, serving the same three-star general as a civilian employee? She nagged the life out of her prince to get her way, and now look at her!

I absolutely loved my job with US Army Space and Missile Defense Command / Army Forces Strategic Command. Immediately after accepting my position, I started to implement new soldier and family programs, which were always successful, especially with a diverse group of people who helped me in pretty much every program.

I am always amazed at how God would send people to help my work, and it was a true joy. I really hated to retire from my dream job, but for some reason, I felt it was time, so I retired on September 30, 2017. I am glad I did, even though I do miss doing things. Every year, I hosted special events and activities that brought me many great memories.

Nobody can tell me there is no God and that it was just a coincidence due to my hard work. I believe every beat of our journey was with God, even when we didn't know God was with us. Without God's protection, his provision, and his forgiveness, we would not have come to where we are. Every day, every hour, and every moment, we praise him and give thanks to him, who is our Savior.

> 2 Corinthians 9:8 And God is able to make all grace abound toward you; that ye, always having all sufficiency in all things, may abound to every good work:

CHAPTER 8

Longing to Hold My Baby in My Arms

> Blessed be the God and Father of our Lord Jesus Christ, the Father of mercies and God of all comfort, who comforts us in all our affliction so that we will be able to comfort those who are in any affliction with the comfort with which we ourselves are comforted by God. (2 Corinthians 1:3–4)

(This chapter was the most difficult to write because it was during the most heartfelt time in our lives. Please have plenty of tissues ready if you are an emotional person.)

It was time for my husband to report to his first duty station since returning to the States after almost four years serving in the Republic of Korea. We were all packed and ready to leave his grandparents' home the next day, and it was September 29, I believe. I felt my stomach tightening, and I noticed a discharge of light blood.

My husband took me to see our family doctor, and he told us that my baby had died in the womb. "How can this be?" I asked the doctor who examined me. My baby was kicking in the morning, and I felt his life in my body all through the night and all day. But the doctor said we need to prepare for the delivery of a dead baby as soon as possible. I was escorted to a hospital room in preparation for a delivery, and my water broke, but there was no sign of a dead baby coming out of my womb. Doctors waited for almost two days, but there was no sign of delivery.

It was October 1, and I was transferred to another hospital where doctors were waiting for me to arrive to start immediate surgery to remove a baby, which had died in my womb. After my water broke, poison began spreading into my body. I was in bad shape, and I was ready to die. The night before being transferred to a hospital in Gainesville, Georgia, I knew something was very wrong and that I might die, and I did not have the will to live after losing my baby.

I remember seeing my son through my hospital room window. He was waving his little hands and calling me while my husband was holding him by the window. He was only two and a half years old. Many thoughts were going through my mind:

What will happen to him when I die?
Who will raise my son, my precious son?
Would his stepmother be nice to him?
Would she take care of my son as if he is her son?
What if she is mean to my son and mistreats him for all his childhood?

My mind was traveling a thousand miles a minute again as I looked at my son waving his little hands by the window. I didn't want to show him my tears, and my thoughts kept coming back to remind me I must live. I must raise that boy to become a man.

The next day, after being transferred to another hospital for surgery to remove a dead baby, Sam sat next to my hospital bed as I was asking him to marry a nice woman who will take good care of our son. I remember telling him to marry my friend who is a registered nurse in Korea. "She would be a good mother to my son. She was the one who taught me how to give a bath and feed a baby. I know she'll be nice to my son," I said. My husband would not budge and give in. He said, "I am not going to marry anybody, and I only want you because I love you."

My heart was aching more, and I just wanted to cry and cry. Why is this happening to me? I am so very young, and so much life is ahead of me, but it is about to be cut short in my twenties. Why am I not being allowed to raise my son, my new baby, take care of my husband, and live the American dream I've always dreamed of?

His love encouraged me to sign the paper for doctors to perform a surgery to remove a dead baby from my womb and to save me. Sam said it was a long day and a long night because the surgery took a very long time. I don't remember how long it took, but I remember hearing that it took many hours, and I lost most of the blood in my body.

I needed to receive a blood transfusion, but my body was rejecting it. After several tries, the doctor said there's not much they can do other than hope and pray that I will be strong enough to make it through day by day and hour by hour. I remember having a nurse in my room for twenty-four hours for several days. As I was getting better, the nurse kept checking on me every hour instead of staying with me. I also remember so many painkiller shots, and one time a nurse was crying and said there was no place for her to put a needle in my body because of too many shots. I had three holes in my stomach and a breathing tube and wasn't able to get out of bed. But I was determined to live for my husband and my son, and I wanted to take care of them.

It had been about ten days since the surgery, and my husband had to report to his new duty station in a few days. His commander gave him two weeks of additional leave before his report day to take care of his family. My husband told the doctor that he did not want to leave me behind without him being there to take care of me. He asked the doctor to release me from the hospital so he could take me with him to his new duty station.

The doctor told us that they had wanted to keep me in the hospital for at least two to three more weeks to recover completely that and all stitches need to be removed. The doctors had to leave my stomach open when surgery was completed, and as I was getting better, he would put a few more stitches in every day.

As I was being discharged from the hospital, the doctor put in a few last stitches before he let me go. The doctor showed my husband what he needed to do every day to care for my wound to ensure it would heal properly without infection. If it got infected, I would have lots of issues, and I could die. He did an amazing job taking care of me every day.

After we reported to his new unit, Sam Jr. and I stayed in a hotel room, while my husband went to work and looked for a place to live. He would come to check on us with food as often as he could. The only thing that was helpful to him was that we were staying on base at a hotel not too far from his office. It was a very difficult time for him, I am sure, and it was hard for a two-and-a-half-year-old boy to stay in a hotel room with a sick and helpless mother. Sam Jr. could not go outside because there was no one to watch him. If he went outside and I was lying in bed, I couldn't do much for him. Sometimes he needed to use the bathroom, and I needed to lift him up and put him on the toilet or help him to reach the toilet bowl, but I wasn't able to lift him. When he realized that I was struggling to lift him, he tried not to bother me. He waited until Daddy came and put him on a toilet.

I cried many times, not because I was sad, though I was sad, but because of his caring and thoughtful spirit at such a young age. How could I ever think of dying and leaving him? Once again, my desire to live consumed my heart. I wanted to see him grow up to become a thoughtful man just like his daddy. Without knowing there is a God, every day in my heart, I was asking, "Dear God, if you are really there, help me to live and take care of my family." I truly believe God heard my prayers, even though I did not know God at the time. "Thank you, God, for your mercy and grace to save my family and me!"

Every morning when Daddy went to work, Sam Jr. would cry, wanting to go with him. I can still hear him crying, "I want my daddy! I want my daddy!" and it was very heartbreaking for all of us. We would tell him that when

Daddy comes from work, then he can go outside to play, and he will bring some candies. He would patiently wait for Daddy to return from work so he could play outside, have something to eat, and also use the bathroom.

To this day, I don't know how my husband was able to do what he did. I thank God for him every day, and I owe him everything, including my life. Sam Jr. did not bother me much, knowing that I could not move fast or pick him up.

I also remember very clearly a dream while we were still in a hotel room. Every night when I fell asleep, I would have a dream that somebody was trying to cover my whole body with a white sheet, and I was fighting not to be covered up. Every night I had the same dream of being covered up with a white sheet, and I would fight, then I heard angels singing the "Hallelujah" chorus. I would wake up with cold sweats and became afraid that I was going to die after all. I fought hard every night with the same dream over and over and would wake up with cold sweats again and again. During this time, I wasn't even a Christian, but for some reason, I knew the heavenly voices singing the "Hallelujah" chorus were angels. I think I won that fight because I am still here and writing my stories.

Thank God!

We finally moved into a nice trailer outside Gate 5 of Fort Gordon, Georgia, located on Highway 78 called Mars Trailer Park. Our trailer was furnished, and we didn't have anything in those days. I mean, we had absolutely nothing. We had a few suitcases with our clothing and his army uniforms, and that was it. We later went to the army exchange (PX) store and bought a rice cooker and some paper plates, plastic bowls, and some other stuff that we needed. We really needed a rice cooker because I was a lousy cook. A Korean wife who can't cook rice on a stove has got to be a lousy cook, and I was. We also went to a thrift store and bought some drinking glasses. I remember I still have one with us.

I was able to see the army OB-GYN doctor whenever I needed to see him. The doctor was a great friend of one of the doctors who performed surgery on me, and they had gone to medical school together. Until this day from time to time, I would pray for both doctors for their children that God will bless them for being so kind to me. I was recovering pretty well and gradually adapted into the army family life.

However, emotionally, I was very deeply discouraged, and I had no one to talk to. I longed to hold my new baby and kept wondering what happened to him. The doctor told us we had a baby boy with average weight for that length of pregnancy. I felt so ashamed to my in-laws that I wasn't able to carry the full term of my pregnancy and wasn't able to present them with a new grandson. I would never be able to bring them more grandchildren. I had become a barren woman who could no longer live as a real woman and produce more children.

I cried alone almost every day, and sometimes I would think that I was pregnant again. I would feel a baby moving and kicking in my stomach, but I knew it couldn't happen. The doctors had told me so, but I did not want to believe them.

We lived in a furnished trailer for about a year, and then we bought a two-bedroom brick house in Augusta,

Georgia. It was not a huge house, but it was ours, even though we had to make mortgage payments every month. We loved our house, and Sam Jr. started kindergarten at Southgate Baptist Christian School. Every morning, under the hot sun, I worked on our front yard to turn the soil, pull weeds, and plant tufts of grass section by section. I made the yard beautiful. I don't know why I spent so much time on it, but later our grass really looked great.

Sam Jr. graduated from kindergarten, and that same year on one Sunday morning, as the pastor was giving the usual invitation after his sermon, Sam Jr. said, "Mommy, I am going to the front and accept Jesus to come into my heart." I watched him as he was walking down the aisle to meet someone to lead him to Christ as his Lord and Savior. I cried and thanked God for giving me this moment to witness him growing up and wanting to have Jesus in his heart. It was one of the most joyous moments in my life to see him growing up with such a gentle spirit.

During his kindergarten year, he memorized forty-five verses, and he tried so hard to make all *A*s. We're so proud of him, and we always have been and always will.

> He that hath the Son hath life, and he that hath not the Son of God hath not life. These things have I written unto you that believe on the name of the Son of God; that ye may know that ye have eternal life and that ye may believe on the name of the Son of God that ye may know that ye have eternal life and that ye may believe on the name of the Son of God. (1 John 5:12–13)

Photo above: This was our first house. We bought it in
1977 when we lived in Augusta, Georgia (Fort Gordon).

CHAPTER 9

It Was Not Ramen and Coke

Therefore I say unto you. Take no thought for your life, what ye shall eat, or what ye shall drink; nor yet for your body, what ye shall put on. Is not the life more than meat, and the body than raiment? Behold the fowls of the air: for they sow not, neither do they reap, nor gather into barns; yet your heavenly Father feedeth them. Are ye not much better than they? (Matthew 6:25–26)

When we first moved into the trailer park outside Fort Gordon, Georgia, Gate 5. there were several Korean women who lived in the same neighborhood, and most of them worked at the local cookie factory. One Korean woman in particular lived right next to us, and her husband was a senior noncommissioned officer with no children. She said she gets paid one hundred dollars every Friday after taxes. I thought that was lots of money for four Fridays in a month, so I thought to myself I should go earn myself a hundred dollars every Friday working in a cookie factory too.

I asked my husband if it was okay for me to get a job at a cookie factory and earn my one hundred dollars every Friday. He immediately said no. He said he wanted his wife to stay home to take care of our son and take care of him and that I need fully recover from a major surgery. I wasn't happy with his answer, so I started to nag him every chance I had and tell him what we could do with four hundred dollars every month. After about three months of nagging day and night, he reluctantly said yes. I drove to the cookie factory, applied for a job, and got hired on the spot.

I was so excited and found a sitter for Sam Jr. who lived in the same trailer park. So here I was, getting up at dawn, dropping him off at a sitter, and rushing to work by 6:45 a.m. I am not a morning person at all, and it was always a struggle for me to get up early, even in my school days, but four hundred dollars a month sure sounded good, so I was motivated to get up early.

The first few days were okay because people took me around and showed me how things worked. I thought to myself, *Yeah, I can do what they do.* And later I was on my own to pack cookies in a box that was wrapped in a plastic paper. I had to pack cookies nice and neat in a box while I was making the boxes. The cardboard boxes were flat, so I had to shape them into a box and then tape them and then fill the boxes with the cookies coming out of machine faster than I could blink my eyes.

To my surprise, I would pack two hands full of cookies in a box, and about five hands full of cookies would fall on the floor. It was out of control. I couldn't keep up, so I just sat on the floor and let all the cookies fall off from the machine. A supervisor came and started screaming on top of her lungs while yelling at me. "What the hell are you doing, you dumb *%#!" I told her that I couldn't keep up and that she would need to slow down the machine or send someone to help me. She said everybody else was working by themselves and I must do it alone too.

Finally, a week went by, and she realized that I wasn't able to handle the job, so she sent me to do other odd jobs and to help out other packers. Just as I was getting used to it, she told me to do something else. I just had it with her mean attitude. So I looked at her and said, "You pay me $2.65 an hour, and you run me like I am your horse." By this time, she just had it with me too.

She motioned me to follow her, and I did. She gave me a broom to sweep the floor and stack cardboard boxes, telling me to tape them and saying "This is a $2.65 an hour job, and you better do it." She said this and walked away. I thought about it for a few seconds and figured out how much I had to pay for a baby sitter and how much I would have in my hand after other expenses such as gas and lunch. To my disappointment, it sure wasn't a hundred dollars a week. I walked toward the exit door of the factory.

The supervisor started yelling at me. "Where the heck are you going?" I replied, "I am going home to my baby so that you can keep my $2.65 an hour job b*%#!" and I clocked out. She yelled at me again, telling me that I would never find another job in America if I walked out. I yelled back to her, "Do you wanna see?" and walked out and never went back. Later my paycheck came in the mail, but it sure wasn't a hundred dollars.

I stayed home for a while and found another job at a cotton mill. The pay was more than the cookie factory, but it was a disastrous job for me. This job required me to feed a machine to weave blue jean fabrics. After two weeks of training, I was still unable to keep up, so I told my supervisor I couldn't do it and walked out again.

A few weeks later, I drove around to find another job that might pay me a hundred dollars a week, and I got hired at McDonald's for flipping burgers. This was a little easier, but I had to spend more time driving to and from work, so yes, I walked out again after I asked my supervisor to give me more hours and he said no, not until I learn more. After a while, I drove around again and stepped into a seafood restaurant, where I got hired to be a hostess and to seat customers when they came in. This was a little more suited for me, and I did all right for a few days, and it didn't seem to be too difficult until the weekend. Every weekend, the front lobby would be packed with seafood lovers, and it was stressful to find seats for them without double seating customers in the wait staff section.

Yes, I walked out but didn't say anything to anybody. I got in my car, drove around for about an hour, and came back to work. My supervisor and other hostesses asked me what happened, and where I went. I told my supervisor that it was too many people and too stressful to seat them all, so I drove around until the lobby was cleared from seafood lovers.

She said she was worried about me, not knowing what happened to one of her employees. She asked me not just to walk out but come to her for help. I don't know why, but she was very good to me. Later she promoted me to be a waitress against her supervisor's advice not to promote me because I wouldn't be able to handle it. To everyone's surprise, I was their best waitress for almost four years. I won every contest they ran, including a round trip to the Road Atlanta 500 for two. Sam Jr. and I went to see racing, and we had a great time.

But being a waitress wasn't easy either. The biggest difficulty in being a waitress was learning all types of drinks and cocktail brands. It was about my fourth week into being a waitress; again, the restaurant was packed with seafood lovers. As usual, I greeted customers at my table and asked if they would like to order any cocktails or appetizers before ordering their dinners.

Everyone ordered their favorite drinks, and one gentleman asked me to bring him a ramen and Coke. I thought it was very strange that he wanted ramen and Coke from an American seafood restaurant, asking for Chinese noodles and Coke before dinner. And I didn't even know if we had Chinese noodles on the menu, but maybe it was a special item, and the customer was hungry.

I came into the kitchen to ring up the order, but there were no keys on the computer, so I yelled out to the kitchen expediter and asked him if he would cook some ramen noodles fast. He was confused and yelled back at me that we weren't a Chinese restaurant, and we didn't have such an item. Then everyone in the kitchen started to laugh. I was upset because people were laughing at me again.

Many times, they would laugh at me with no apparent reason other than me being an Asian woman to them. It was very frustrating for me that sometimes the young dishwasher or table bussers were acting stupid every time they passed by me and made Chinese motions. I was to the point of getting sick of their dumb demeanor, but I paid no attention to them and just kept on working. But an expediter yelling and laughing at me was a little too much, so I cried.

Shortly after that, my supervisor walked in and asked what was going on. I told her about the two couples at my table, where one gentleman wanted ramen and Coke. I gave him a glass of Coke, and now I needed ramen for him before ordering his dinner, but the kitchen staff was laughing at me again. I sensed that she tried not to laugh along with others, and she held my hand and took me to the bar and had a bartender prepare a rum and Coke for me to deliver to my customer. I was sure he said ramen and Coke.

When I went back to my table and told that kind gentleman that I thought he had ordered ramen and Coke, we all laughed hard for a long time, and I finally got what rum and Coke was. As I look back in my life of those days, I may not have known many things, but God was there to help me to learn and overcome many challenges. And most of all, I learned to ignore the harassment of ignorant people who knew no better than to discriminate against different nationalities.

Nowadays, people are a little more aware of different cultures, and many appreciate the Asian cultures especially. Almost every day when I go out, I am faced with people being skeptical about me because I am an Asian woman, not to mention an older Asian woman.

Although some may dislike Asian people in general, most people have been kind to me and accepted me as a friend.

Often, they're surprised to see my work ethics, my speaking abilities, or my creativity and willingness to jump in to help. I love to be engaged with new projects or revive programs that have been buried or were never there.

Whenever I needed to build a team to do something, I recognized that God would always send people of diverse groups to run the project with me. It's so amazing how God has worked through other people's lives to equip me to do a better job. It always makes me humble in God's amazing grace and his never-ending love and mercy. How did I get here? It's all because of the cross of Jesus, and I thank him every moment.

> But seek ye first the kingdom of God, and his righteousness; and all these things shall be added unto you. Take therefore no thought for the morrow: for the morrow shall take thought for the things of itself. Sufficient unto the day is the evil thereof. (Matthew 6:33–34)

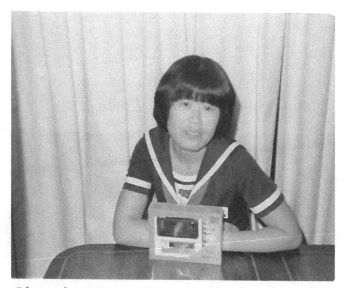

Photo above: Me with the first-place prizes for the best waitress contest. I won a camera and trip for two to Road Atlanta 500. Sam Jr. and I went and had a great time and were treated very nice.

CHAPTER 10

A Beautiful Bride

O magnify the Lord with me, and let us
exalt His name together. (Psalm 34:3)

Photo above: Our wedding day.

It's been a few years since we had somewhat settled into
our new home in Augusta, Georgia. We were busy as a
working army family. I was a waitress, and Sam was moving up in his rank while Sam Jr. was in kindergarten. We
didn't have much, but we were a happy army family. The

one thing I had in my heart for a very long time was yet to happen. I wanted to be a bride. By then, I had been nagging Sam all the time to marry me. His answers were always the same. "You are my wife, and we've been married several years now, and it is time that you get used to being my wife." My answer was always "But I don't feel like I am married because I have never worn a white wedding gown with a veil and walked down the aisle with you."

As time went on, I continued to nag him day and night, saying "Will you marry me?" As usual, his answer was always pretty much the same. "We are married," or sometimes he would say, "No, I can't marry you because I am already married." I believed every girl's dream was to become a bride and wear a beautiful white wedding gown and veil while walking down the aisle to meet her husband-to-be. In this case, I was no less a dreamer than any girl or woman.

We got married by obtaining a marriage certificate from the American Embassy signed by the mayor of the City of Seoul. We heard so many stories about the day when we would receive our marriage certificate. But all the stories I heard never came close to my expectations. We didn't exchange wedding vows with each other, but I remember signing my name on many pages.

Then Sam came back from a little window where he had been talking to somebody and said, "Let's go home." I looked at him. "I thought we're going to get married today," I asked. "Yes, we are married, and you are now my wife, and your last name is Bertling," he replied.

Photo above: Our wedding party. Maid of honor, Ms. Vivian Brown; flower girl, Miranda Ford; best man, SSG Herbert Hernandez; ring Bearer, Sam Bertling Jr.; Pastor Bill Rice in the center from Southgate Baptist Church, Augusta, GA.

"Well, I don't feel I am married because all I did was sign a bunch of papers. I am not going home until we are married," I replied to Sam. My voice was firm because I was told we were going to the embassy to get married since all our paperwork was now complete.

Sam insisted that we were married, and I was now his wife. I didn't feel I was married, other than having a military identification card showing that he is my sponsor. As my nagging went on to have a church wedding, one day he finally said he would marry me. How excited I was!

Then the first thing I needed to do was find the white wedding gown of my dreams and a veil. I also needed to find a minister who would marry us. I went to my ladies

Sunday school teacher and asked her if her husband would marry me and Sam since he was the church pastor. The following week, she said her husband told her no because he doesn't perform second marriage ceremonies. She explained this means he does not marry people who are getting married for the second time or divorced couples. So Sam and I both went to the pastor's office and explained the whole nine yards of how we were married but never exchanged vows. He finally said yes, that he would perform our wedding ceremony.

I was so excited. I went and bought a beautiful white wedding gown and veil and asked my supervisor to be my maid of honor. Sam invited his friend to be the best man. Sam Jr. would be the ring bearer, and our next-door neighbor's daughter was to be a flower girl. Every detail had been set, and Sam worked all night so he could have a day off to get married to his wife, to whom he was already married on paper. Our wedding day came. Oh, how excited I was.

Sam and I walked the aisle together and exchanged our wedding vows. After that, we heard the pastor say we were now husband and wife.

We had the beautiful church wedding that I had always wanted. Our wedding was not a large one like we could see on television, but it was a beautiful day with a beautiful wedding with wonderful friends and great reception at our house. I cherish that day and am so thankful to the pastor of Southgate Baptist Church, Dr. Bill Rice, who officiated our wedding. I had finally reached my American dream of riding on a white horse with my prince to Sunrise Avenue to live happily ever after, as God was with us all throughout those years as we grew to maturity as an army family.

This is a great mystery: but I speak concerning Christ and the church. Nevertheless, let every one of you in particular so love his wife even as himself; and the wife see that she reveres her husband. (Ephesians 5:32–33)

CHAPTER 11

Legacy 4 Korean War Veterans Foundation

But this I say, he which soweth sparingly shall reap also sparingly; and he which soweth bountifully shall reap also bountifully. Every man according as he purposeth in his heart, so let him give; not grudgingly, or of necessity: for God loveth a cheerful giver. (2 Corinthians 9:6–9)

Sharing hot meals with Korean War veterans has been my childhood ambition. It was during my elementary school years. In the city, there was a poor man who lived on the street here and there as city officials pushed him around.

As time went on, I heard that he was severely wounded during the Korean War and lost all his family and had no place to go. In front of him was a small broken bowl that he used to beg for food. To this day, I don't know why my heart was so drawn to him. Sometimes I saw him sit outside my school gate, and I remember seeing children laughing at him and throwing rocks at him.

For some reason, I wanted to give him the food that my mother had packed for my lunch. But it wasn't much at all, and mostly it was just barley with some beans. Whenever I had my lunch and if he was sitting outside my school gate, during my lunchtime, when nobody was watching, I would run to him and pour my food into his bowl and then run back to class. I didn't want anybody to see what I was doing. I didn't want my mother to be upset because I gave away my lunch to a homeless man.

We were all told not to get close to people who lived on the streets. Since I never had any money or any food that was good enough, I had always hoped that one day, if I had enough money in my hands, I would like to buy him a hot meal. I can't imagine how cold it was in the winter and how hungry he would be.

Later, during a bitterly cold winter, I learned that he had died on the street. I never shared this with anybody, but I feel so sad to this day. He had no place to go, no food to eat, and no one to love him or anyone for him to love. Even though my family didn't have much, at the end of the day, I could go home and have some hot soup that my mother had prepared for us. Then I could sleep in a room, but that homeless Korean War veteran lived on the street day and night until he died.

That made me always wish that one day when I had enough money to spare, I would share a hot meal with a Korean War Veteran. That thought remained in my head all my life, even though I can't say I ever had much money in my hands. If I did, it was always needed for my family. So pretty much, I kept that thought in my head on a back burner, hoping one day I would have that opportunity.

In the summer of 2006, I had a golden opportunity to share a hot meal at a Korean restaurant with not one but six Korean War veterans with two of their wives who attended a free lunch in their honor. In the following year, it happened again, but the attendance grew more than double and then grew again in the third year.

My husband, Sam, and I have to move the next luncheon to a local Italian restaurant due to the number of attendance growing beyond our expectation, and that Korean restaurant was no longer able to accommodate a large crowd size. It was a very exciting time because I had always hoped to share a hot meal with Korean War veterans, but we're having a room full of them with their families, our community leaders, and a high-ranking military general officers as our guest speaker.

Since then, the luncheon program has grown beyond anyone's expectations as we continued to host annual lunches paid out of our own pockets. After much prayers and consideration for expenses, as attendances grew larger each year, the Legacy 4 Korean War Veterans Foundation came to life as a 501 (c)(3), a nonprofit organization in January 2011.

In November 2012, my husband and I sponsored nine Korean War veterans and three guardians to revisit Korea with all expenses paid. All nine veterans who took this trip shared their testimonies about how the trip brought a profound impact on their lives and healing to their war-torn memories for more than six decades.

Photo above: Welcome home water cannon salute by the Huntsville Fire Department on November 14, 2012, as an airplane carries our Korean War veterans back from a Revisit Korea trip. Later I received this photo but cannot remember who sent to me.

Photo above: On November 6, 2019, N. AL Veterans and Fraternal Orgs Coalition presented us with the Madison County Veteran Organization of the Year at the annual AUSA Redstone/Huntsville Chapter Veterans Week dinner.

Each year, as we hosted the annual luncheon, the event turned out to be better, and more guests joined us to honor the Korean War veterans. Our mission honoring the Korean War veterans will continue as long as we have resources and the community members' support, and there is a need for it.

In November 2019, Legacy 4 Korean War Veterans Foundation was recognized as Veteran Organization of the Year by the North Alabama Veterans Fraternal Organizations Coalition. It was a tremendous honor as we are privileged to serve those who have served, but most importantly, our resources and volunteers who support our mission anytime we need their help.

Photo above: In 2016, the City of Huntsville Officials unanimously voted to name the Old Madison Pike newly rebuilt bridge to Korean War Veterans Memorial Bridge. Beverly Lowe worked hard for this.

While we are eager to honor our veterans with every opportunity we have, there are so many who never made it home to their loved ones. Countless families are still waiting to hear what happened to their loved ones who went to war when they were so young. Many parents died without ever knowing what happened to their son or daughter. My prayers are always with their families wherever they may be, that God's amazing grace will give them comfort and peace through our Lord that their loved ones' sacrifices are not in vain.

> And we indeed justly; for we receive the due reward of our deeds: but this man hath done nothing amiss. And he said unto Jesus, LORD, remember me when

thou comest into thy kingdom. 43And
Jesus said unto him, Verily I say unto thee,
Today shalt thou be with me in paradise.
(Luke 23:41–43)

CHAPTER 12

Honors and Recognitions

And whatsoever ye do, do it heartily, as
to the Lord, and not unto men; Knowing
that of the Lord ye shall receive the reward
of the inheritance: for ye serve the Lord
Christ. (Colossians 3:23–24)

Through my volunteer work and as a Department of the
Army Civilian employee, I have received numerous awards
and recognitions by the army's top-ranking general officers
and commanders. It makes me feel that I was accepted into
their mission as a team member, and it gives me tremendous gratitude.

The recognitions also bring people to draw themselves
close to me. When I was growing up, on many occasions, I
was not accepted because I was a child of a poor family, and
it was very painful then. But as a grown-up, I never pushed
myself in to be accepted by anybody or any group because
I've always thought to myself if they reject me, that is not
my loss. Rather, it is their loss because I know I would be a
team player. Even if anybody hires me to be a ditch digger,
I know I will be the best and the most creative ditch digger

anybody could ever have. Yes, I am confident in this statement. So I don't get so heartbroken as when I was a child. I will keep my head up and will keep walking for something better.

Receiving awards and recognitions adds to life's treasures too. My husband and my son are very proud of my recognitions for the work I perform. However, deep down in my heart, I have always had guilty feelings because I left my homeland and my family to live my own life. Not a day goes by without thinking about my siblings in Korea.

Often I wonder if they were thinking about their baby sister, who was a rebellious girl, and how her laughing was so loud that it carried outside the family house for the whole village people to hear? Women in my days were supposed to laugh quietly and not so loud so everyone outside the house could hear.

I wondered if my nieces and nephews still remember they once had an aunt who carried them on her back when they were babies? I carried the first three children of my brothers on my back, and many times they wetted my back. We never had disposable diapers, only cloth diapers, so naturally, they wet the cloth diapers and then to my back.

My heart aches when I think about how hard my two older brothers and an older sister's lives as it was very challenging financially, emotionally, and physically trying to make a living and to raise their children. I know they worked very hard to ensure all their children receive education that they have never received, and that was their priority.

I also often think about if their lives would be better if I invited them all to come to the United States to live with me? I saw many Korean women who were married to military members and brought their entire families to the States and lived in the same house until they could be on their own. Many had money to own their businesses, and many didn't have ways and means to support themselves and brought on a heavy burden for the soldier to take care of his entire in-laws in an army government housing.

While many families were successful, many others were not, and marriages ended in a divorce, or many returned to Korea because they could not handle the challenges they have to overcome.

In the late 1970s, my oldest brother's wife wrote to me and asked me to invite my mother to the States, and then she could invite my brother and his family to come too, and so on. I thought about that a lot to this day.

At that time, when I received her letter, we were not in any shape to bring them to the States to live with us. We didn't have extra income. We had our only child in a Christian school that we have to pay tuition every month out of our own pockets. Not to mention we have to take him to school and pick him up afterward. To save gas money, most of the days, I stayed at school as a volunteer to clean bathrooms and church sanctuary after the school events, mopped the hallways, and also helped teachers to grade children's test papers

I thought if my family couldn't make it in Korea where they speak the same language and it was a place of their own, how would they make it in the States with a language barrier and no money? I would have to be with them all the time, and then my life would be consumed with taking care of them and sending their four children to school while taking care of my mother too.

Before I wrote back to my sister-in-law, I thought about it day and night for several months. It still hurts me that I wasn't able to bring them.

If I started to bring my brother's family, what about my other siblings? How would I take care of them? How would my husband and my son handle it? To take care of my siblings, I would have to neglect my husband and my only son. My son did not ask me to bring him into this world, but his dad and I did. Would it be fair that his mother neglects him to take care of his uncles, aunts, and their children? Also, would it be fair to my husband, who thought he was marrying me and not the entire in-laws who don't even speak the same language?

I have always thought about these things and felt very guilty because I left to follow my prince, whom I waited for most of my childhood until he came.

While I am looking back and thinking about how my life would have turned out if I had brought my older siblings to the States, would I have achieved all that I have become? I am a thousand percent sure I would not be where I am today. Would I still be married to my husband of close to fifty years? It's not that my husband would not have taken care of my siblings and me since we both promised to each other for richer or poorer, in sickness and in health, till death do us apart. But I can't imagine the burdens I would have loaded onto his shoulders all his life.

And for my son, he would have to go along with Mom and Dad, but I also can't imagine how much pressure he would have lived through seeing his mom and dad always struggling to take care of my large family. Even though in a way, we did want to have a large family, but it was with our children, not my siblings.

I am eternally grateful for my life and how it has become, but forever deep in my heart, I feel guilty because of knowing that my siblings struggled and I did not invite them to come to the United States of America to live with us. I think about this a lot. If they came, would they have been more successful than they were in Korea?

I would never know, but I believe they did great in raising their children. All of them are very successful in their own right as they raised their children. My only hope is that my nephews and nieces will never blame me for not bringing their parents to live in the States so they, too, could have lived and be educated in the United States.

All these thoughts are in my head, but I am almost sure nothing would have turned out the way it has for my siblings and me.

My first visit to Korea was in the fall of 1985, which was almost ten years later after I left. During that time, my oldest brother and his family still lived in the same village. And my last visit was in October 1992 for my first nephew's wedding. That's when I learned that my oldest brother had left the little village where I grew up during my teenage years to a city apartment with a modern-day setup, Even though I understand they wanted to live in a city with modern systems such as indoor kitchen, bathrooms, electricity, etc., in a way, I feel very sad that he gave up the house that he built himself with his own hands with my father to bring his bride when he got married. Since they are no longer living in that village, I lost the desire to return to Korea.

Nevertheless, I dream of my homeland every night and day where my life began as a young girl full of life's ambitions that I never told anyone. I guess now I must forget all as life goes on and accept things as it is meant to be, but I have not been able to do that. At least not yet, or I never will. My daily prayers for them is that God will bless them and their children and know our Savior, the Lord Jesus Christ, who paid the ransom for our sins.

My siblings may never know how I feel about not bringing them to the United States and all my life's accomplishments, but I know how difficult their lives were in the early days. I hope they will all understand and find in their hearts to forgive me for choosing to live my own life.

Though they might think life has afforded me the best, which is true, my husband and I paid our dues too. It wasn't always easy moving around in military life. I have to learn to carry on our lives when my husband was gone so many times, including during the Gulf War Desert Shield / Desert Storm in the early 1990s and a one-year tour of duty to Korea in 1988. If it weren't for my husband's diligent way of taking care of us, we would not be where we are today. He was always there, even though he was out of the country, and he provided us with his firm guidance for Sam Jr. and me to follow, but he gave me the freedom to try out my way. Yes, there were many things I learned the hard way.

And for Sam Jr., he was always above average. Even at his young age, he was very caring and thoughtful and always considered others. There were many times we had to tell him no because we didn't have the money or it was something we didn't believe in. He took his father's place when my husband was gone and tried to comfort me when I cried.

So many times, I wish I've known at least one-tenth of what I know now when he was in high school that would have prepared him to go to college instead of joining the United States Navy, or I could have trained him to play better baseball.

Overall, we are very proud of Sam Jr. for his achievements in life and service to our country. He has been on his own since he graduated from high school and never asked us for money. He would talk to his dad about things as father and son would discuss, but he supports himself very well.

My husband and Sam Jr. play baseball with the Atlanta Braves legends in January of each year. This is the best time for both father and son, and I enjoy watching them having so much fun playing baseball together.

God has been very good to my family more than I have ever dreamed of and to me. God has sent me many friends who mentor me along the way, and they taught me to become a polished public speaker.

I don't deserve what God has given me. I am thankful for everything and cherish every moment. When I was growing up, America was so far away, but yet America was so close in my heart. Nowadays, Korea, my homeland, is so far away but so close in my heart. I will never forget my roots, and I will always carry my dignity as a Korean woman. Every day is a new day, and I am grateful for living the American dream. I pray every day that all my siblings will know Christ, our Lord, who paid the penalty of our sins on the old rugged cross.

More than forty years ago, my husband Sam and I rode into the Sunrise Avenue together after that first kiss, and we've experienced many of life's fun and exciting events and also many challenges. Some were great, and some were not so, but we've made it through our journeys.

Now we are walking into the Sunset Boulevard, looking back how it was then and thanking God for his steadfast love and mercy more than we can ever dream possible. If we were to live our lives all over again, we would change nothing, but perhaps we would serve God more, who is and has been our shelter and our guiding light.

All my awards and recognitions, I won't be able to take with me to eternity, but my heart will never cease to be amazed by God's infinite mercy and grace in Jesus Christ, my Lord.

> Now the God of peace, that brought again from the dead our LORD Jesus, that great Shepherd of the sheep, through the blood of the everlasting covenant, Make you perfect in every good work to do his will, working in you that which is well pleasing in his sight, through Jesus Christ; to whom be glory forever and ever. Amen. (Hebrews 13:20–21)

Photo above: I received one of the most prestigious
awards in the Madison County on November 4, 2019.
Brigadier General Bob Drolet's Service to Veterans Award.
In the picture from left to right are Rhonda Sutton,
me, Sam, and Steve Below. Rhonda is VP and Steve is
President of AUSA Redstone/Huntsville Chapter.

Photo above: Lieutenant General David L. Mann, Commander of US Army Space and Missile Defense Command / Army Forces Strategic Command presented me with the Employee of the Year in April 2016.

CHAPTER 13

KC's Awards

KC's awards throughout her volunteer career and as a US Army civilian employee.

Civilian Employee Awards:
- Civilian Employee of the Year
- Meritorious Civilian Service Award
- Superior Civilian Service Award
- Commander's Civilian Service Medal (2)
- Commander's Award for Public Service Medal (2)

Employment History:
- 2009 to 2017: Soldier and Family Program Manager
- (Retired from this position)
- 2008 to 2009: Special Emphasis Program Manager
- 2005 to 2008: Executive Assistant
- 2003 to 2005: Management Assitant
- 2002 to 2003: Community Volunteer Program Coordinator

- 2001 to 2002: Army Family Team Building Manager
- 1996 to 2000: Recreation Specialist

Volunteer Awards:
- AUSA Volunteer Family of the Year
- Patriotic Service Awards (2)
- Commander's Award for Public Service (3)
- Numerous Volunteer Awards by General Officers

Volunteer History:
- 2020 to present: President N. AL Veterans and Fraternal Organizations Coalition (NAVFOC)
- 2016 to present: Board member Association of the United States Army Board
- 2016 to 2020: Chaplain N. AL Veterans and Fraternal Organizations Coalition
- 2011 to present: Co-Founder/Secretary Legacy 4 Korean War Veterans Foundation
- 2013–2014: President of Redstone Arsenal Community Women's Club
- 2000–2002: Vice President of the European Protestant Women of the Chapel (PWOC)
- 2001–2002: President of the 100th Area PWOC (Oversaw five local chapters)
- 1997–2000: President, PWOC Hohenfels Chapter

CHAPTER 14

Three Generations of the Bertling family

Photo above: Thomas A. Bertling. Sadly, he departed
us when Sam was only about five years old.

CHAPTER 15

Signs Lost in Interpretation

There hath no temptation taken you but such as is common to man: but God is faithful, who will not suffer you to be tempted above that ye are able; but will with the temptation also make a way to escape, that ye may be able to bear it. (1 Corinthians 10:13)

When I first obtained a driver's license, it wasn't that difficult to pass the written exam and driving test. But afterward, I was on my own while driving. Filling the gas tank and knowing how to park was the most challenging for me. More than a few times, I've asked people to park my car for me if I found space was too tight to park between cars. I won't do it now. I remember I would always look for parking spaces far away from the store, even if I had to take a few extra steps to get to the store to shop. For me, it was easier to park and get out when there were no other vehicles next to where I wanted to park.

Parking was always a struggle for me, and Sam Jr. even asked me why I always parked so far away from the store where we were planning to go shopping. "It's easier for me to park and get out when there are no other cars parked next to me" was always my answer. It took many years for me to learn to put gas in my car, and parallel parking was out of the question.

When we lived in a trailer park, the only way to park your vehicle was to parallel park in front of our trailer gate. But at that time, I didn't even know what parallel parking meant. I would come home, park my car by the gate, and run in the house to let my husband know that my car was out there for him to park. Yes, I tried a few times, but it didn't work, so whenever he was home, he would park the car and fill up the tank. All I had to do was just drive forward.

Anyway, parking was nothing compared to understanding all the traffic signs. Somehow, I passed the written exam, but there were so many other things I needed to learn, especially what each sign meant, even after I got my license and was already driving. Most signs I understood, but some I didn't. As long as I knew the Stop sign, yield, speed limits, red, orange (or yellow), and green lights, that was all I needed to know. At least that was my thinking. While I was a lousy driver, I was also perplexed with signs such as the following:

- Slower Traffic Keep Right
- No U-Turn (but I had to make a U-turn to go where I needed to)
- No Left Turn (if I can't make a left turn, how will I get to go where I need to go?)

It was late one evening when my Korean friend called me while I was working. She said to come over to her house to eat some pig's feet with kimchi, which she had prepared for her friends, and I can come and have my share of it too. That sounded so tasty, and I had never eaten pig's feet with kimchi before, although I heard it was very tasty. It was about ten o'clock in the evening, and yes, I was kind of hungry too, so I told her I would join her. By the time I cleaned my station and got on the I-520 Bobby Jones Expressway, it was about eleven o'clock.

As I was driving down the freeway, there was no traffic, so I was all by myself driving the fifty-five miles per hour speed limit. But it was so strange that evening. No one was in front of me, and no one was behind me when I saw a sign that said Slower Traffic Keep Right. I wondered what that sign meant. I tried to ignore that sign and stayed on the right lane, keeping up with fifty-five. But that sign kept showing up like it was a neon sign that kept flashing at me.

Finally, it clicked in my head. The sign means that if you want to drive the speed limit, you'd stay in the right lane, but if you want to go faster than the speed limit, you would need to get in the left lane. Well, my interpretation was partially correct.

As soon as I got into the left lane and stepped on the gas pedal to about sixty-five to seventy miles per hour, I saw bright blue lights flashing behind me. But I didn't pay any attention because I was not doing anything wrong. I was obeying the traffic sign that said Slower Traffic Keep Right, and I wasn't driving slow. I was driving faster than the speed limit, so I had no reason to stop. I just stayed in the left lane and continued to drive to my friend's house so I could have some of the pig's feet that she had cooked all day for her other friends and me.

Then the bright blue light got closer, and the siren got louder, and the policeman was shouting at me to stop and pull over. *What?* I was thinking. It is the middle of the night, nobody was on the highway, and I am supposed to pull over? I don't think so. So I kept on driving. The voice got much louder, so I finally pulled over. I couldn't figure out what I did wrong. As I looked through the rearview mirror, I saw a state trooper step out of his patrol car. He was yelling at me to step out of my vehicle.

I opened my car door, put out my left foot, and stuck out my head. "Me do wrong, Officer?" I asked. Then he realized that I was an Asian woman who spoke broken English wearing a white pair of shoes. I guess he didn't feel very threatened by my presence, so he came over to me. In the dark, I looked at him with my best innocent face, "What me do wrong, Officer? Me no do wrong, Officer." I was biting my lips while asking him the questions with a totally innocent face as it was somewhat dark. "Why did you change lanes when no one was in front of you?" he asked. "Oh, Officer, me see sign Slower Traffic Keep Right. Me no wanna drive slow. So me changed to left lane. Me go faster," I answered him.

"Officer, me go eat pig's feet at my friend's. She cooked pig's feet all day for me. Me go faster now, okay?" I could tell he was trying to hold himself from laughing at me.

This kind officer explained to me what that sign meant. He said it was meant for drivers to yield to the left, being sure no one was behind me, then get in the left lane to pass vehicles in front of me in the right lane if they were driving under the speed limit. The sign did not mean I could just change the lane to go faster when no one was in front of me. He wanted to be sure that I understood what he was telling me.

"Ma'am, do you understand what I am telling you?" he asked. "Yes, me understand, Officer. Me go fast now on the right lane to my friend's house to eat pig's feet, okay?" I said. "No, no, you do not drive faster. You drive fifty-five and drive safely so you can go eat your friend's pig's feet."

He wanted to make sure that I understood what he was telling me. He also spoke very slowly to me so I would understand what he was telling me. At least that was his thinking, I guess. So he let me off the hook from getting a speeding ticket and told me to drive slow and safely so I would have a chance to have the pig's feet.

A few months went by, and the restaurant was busy again with seafood lovers. I went to a table where two couples were just seated at my station with four glasses of water, and I started to make my usual waitress speech in welcoming them. As I finished the speech, one gentleman looked right into my eyes. "I know you. You are that Asian woman who said 'What me do wrong, Officer.'" It was then that I recognized his voice. Everyone at the table was very quiet, wondering what was going on. Then he said, "Don't let me catch you again!" "Oh no, sir! I won't let you catch me again!"

Everyone had a great dinner and gave me a large tip, and the two ladies told me that I got him good and laughed with me. I guess you could say I took advantage of his kindness. But since I didn't know what that sign meant, I felt I could surely justify that I got away from getting a speeding ticket. However, I've gotten more than my share of speeding tickets through the years. But most people think I drive very slow compared to a few others. I guess you can say I am generally a slow driver. But then, there was another sign that I could never figure out, and it was not what it meant, but why?

One day, I was in a hurry to go pick up Sam Jr. for his swimming lessons at the YMCA. I rushed out of work and tried to get to his sitter's house to pick him up. I came out, and the red light had a sign that said No Left Turn. Then when I went to the next traffic light, it said No U-Turn. I was really in a hurry, and I had already passed two traffic lights. Nothing allowed me to make a turn to get on the highway that I needed to get on. As I was driving through the traffic light trying to make a U-turn, I saw it said No U-Turn, but I made a U-turn anyway while a police car was right behind me. As I was making the U-turn, I could see his face was so surprised to see what I was doing right in front of him. Yes, he turned on his blue lights, and I pulled over.

"Ma'am, may I see your driver's license, registration, and insurance card? Do you know what you just did?" he asked. "Yes, sir. I just made a U-turn because the other traffic light said No Left Turn, and the second light said No U-Turn, but I had to go pick up my son and take him to his swimming lessons. I am really, really in a hurry, Officer. Will you just let me go, please?" I asked with my most innocent face. "You could have gone to the next light a block from where you just made the illegal U-turn. Then you would have been allowed to make turns," he said. Then he said, "I'll let you off this time but drive safe." I was a bit late in taking Sam Jr. to his swimming lessons, but I didn't get a ticket.

I have wondered many times would it work if I tried that nowadays. I am not sure if it would work with my broken accent. Nevertheless, I can confidently say how God forgives his children and overlooks our sins through his Son, Jesus, our Lord.

> In whom we have redemption through his blood, the forgiveness of sins, according to the riches of his grace; Wherein he hath abounded toward us in all wisdom and prudence; Having made known unto us the mystery of his will, according to his good pleasure which he hath purposed in himself: (Ephesians 1:7–10)

Note: Kimchi is a traditional Korean dish of fermented vegetables, the most common of which are napa cabbage and daikon radish. In addition to being served as banchan, called Korean side dishes presented as part of a meal, it can also be used in a variety of cooked dishes. Try it as a sauce for brussel sprouts, with braised short ribs, or in Korean tofu soup. You will always want to have more.

CHAPTER 16

My Closing Thoughts

Let your light so shine before men, that they may see your good works, and glorify your Father which is in heaven. (Matthew 5:16)

This book was written with much prayers and thanksgiving to God, my son, and my husband, who have been my rocks throughout our journeys together.

While the process of this book was coming together, I was very excited and kept asking God to help me and help my publisher. I also felt somewhat apprehensive because I was a bit concerned and insecure about my writings, which you can say is very elementary.

Generally, I am a very secure and confident person in what I do. Perhaps sometimes I can be overconfident, which is one of my weaknesses. This book was much different from the writings I've done in the past because it carries my life's stories to the world and to people I don't know and may never meet.

I offer my prayers for every person who reads this book, that you feel a sense of God's presence in each chapter and receive his amazing grace and mercy in Jesus Christ, our Lord. I ask every person who reads this book to remember (I pray) that God will lead you to this little book to enrich your life. Thank you, and may God bless you always!

These are the three verses I've chosen for this page:

- Matthew 5:16

Years ago, my husband wrote this verse in my birthday card. Ever since then, I kept it in my heart.

- Romans 3:23 "For all have sinned, and come short of the glory of God."
- Romans 3:23 is one of the forty-five verses Sam Jr. memorized when he was in kindergarten. It always reminds me that Jesus paid for my sins.
- Jeremiah 33:3 "Call unto me, and I will answer thee, and show thee great and mighty things, which thou knowest not."
- Jeremiah 33:3 is one of my favorite verses. It always reminds me to call unto God whenever I feel discouraged or have concerns.

My Scrapbook

Before showing you photos of our precious memories, I thought to share an old hymn that I often sing while driving alone or whatever I maybe doing in the house.

"Pass Me Not, O Gentle Savior"

Pass me not, O gentle Savior, Hear my humble cry, While
    on others Thou art calling, do not pass me by; Savior,
    Savior, hear my humble cry, while on others Thou art
    calling, do not pass me by.
Thou the spring of all my comfort, more than life to me,
    whom have I on earth beside Thee, whom in heaven
    but Thee, Savior, Savior, hear my humble cry, while on
    others Thou art calling, do not pass me by.

General Barry R. McCaffrey, US Army Retired

VICTORY DIVISION
May 18, 1992

Dear Mrs. Bertling:

Thank you for your gracious letter of May 6th. Your thoughtfulness in writing and the kindness your words expressed was much appreciated.

It has been an honor to serve with the outstanding soldiers of the 24th ID(M). Certainly, the soldiers of the LRSD rank among the elite in our Division. Their accomplishment of a number of tough missions during Operations Desert Shield and Desert Storm played an important role in that great victory. The leadership and example provided by your husband has been key to the LRSD's superior performance.

Again, thank you for taking the time to write. We appreciate your prayers and support.

Sincerely,

Barry R. McCaffrey
Major General, U.S. Army
Commanding

Mrs. K.C. Bertling
57 Lincoln Avenue
Fort Stewart, Georgia 31313

Photo above: I have always wanted to sing with the army band. On June 27, 2016, I was given a lifetime honor to sing "America the Beautiful" with the United States Army Materiel Command Orchestra for the seventy-fifth anniversary of Redstone Arsenal. You can view my performance on YouTube: https://bit.ly/2Zid2NW

Photo above: Me singing the national anthem at the Annual Atlanta Braves Fantasy Camp Legend versus the Campers in January 2018. It is always a highest honor and privilege to sing the national anthem.

Photos bottom left: Sam Sr. volunteering. *Bottom right:* Sam Jr. serving Thanksgiving dinner for homeless veterans.

Photo above: Sam Jr. and Sam Sr.

Photo above: Me singing the national anthem
at the Command Town Hall Meeting.

Photo above: My nieces and nephews.

Photo above: My oldest nephew with his bride in 1992.

Photo above: My second sister in-law left from back row
with her two daughters and son. My sister is on the right.

Photo above: On the front, in 1992, Sam is leading his Long Range Surveillance Detachment (LRSD) unit to see General Norman Schwarzkopf during the Desert Shield / Desert Storm.

1996 Last day to report to duty as an active duty Soldier

1988 Sam in Korea

Photo above: On September 2016, I served as a Combined Federal Campaign Chairwoman for the entire TN Valley Communities. Kickoff cake-cutting ceremony: *From left to right:* Lieutenant General David L. Mann, keynote speaker, and Major General Allan W. Elliot representing the Army Materiel Command.

Top left: Elementary school friends. *Top Right:* Junior year best friend.

Photo above: My later year friends. *Left top:* with Chae.
Left bottom: with YoungHui. *On the right:* Tammy.

Photo above: Sam Jr.'s drawing when
he was in the kindergarten.

At the Cross
Visit to Kwajalein Atoll for soldiers and families
quality of life assessment trip with the Commanding
General Richard P. Formica in 2012.
There was the cross by the seaside!
O Lord, how great thou art!

A Chance to be Born

ENDORSEMENTS

As a Korean War veteran, I have witnessed the resiliency of the Korean people and their patriotism. KC's incredible journeys to her American dream and her unshakable faith in God will inspire everyone.

Honorable Mario F. Ventura
Retired, the 22nd Judicial Justice
Court District 10 of Louisiana

I spent twenty-seven months in POW Camp #3 in North Korea. KC's passion for honoring Korean War veterans bring healing to all of us who kept the war memories to ourselves.

Corporal Newton Duke
Former POW Korean War Veteran

No matter where you're born and raised, to realize all the goodness that this nation has to offer is everyone's goal in life. Through hard work, devotion to duty, and love of country, KC has done just that. I am very proud to call her my friend, and I am honored to work with her in helping others enjoy this great miracle we call the American Dream. This book delivers KC's inspirational, moving, and uplifting story.

Dr. Joe Fitzgerald
Civilian Aide to Secretary of the Army (N. AL)

KC has invited you to walk through her life's incredible journeys to the American dream from her childhood. Her epic story of life's triumphant victory will inspire your heart and your children. KC is a delightful lady with a compelling and heartwarming story we can all enjoy and celebrate.

Brigadier General Robert Drolet
Retired US Army

This incredible book will give you a heart full of love and pride in being an American. As a little girl who dreamed of living the American dream from the faraway country of the Republic of Korea, KC tells the true beauty of the United States of America.

Command Sergeant Major Robert Whiteford
Retired US Army

Among many things, KC is very passionate about volunteerism and inspiring young people. As KC is living her childhood fairy-tale dream, she and her family strive to serve veterans and to volunteer in the community day in and day out.

Steve Below
President, Association of the United States
Army Redstone/Huntsville Chapter

ABOUT THE AUTHOR

As a young girl, KC dared to dream that one day a dashing young prince will come riding on a white horse, scepter in his hand, a crown on his head with eyes that would make her almost faint. And after the first kiss, he would sweep her away into his adventurous world on Sunrise Avenue to live happily ever after.

Her prince came with a bit of twisted way as he was riding on an army green Jeep, holding an M16 in his hand, army green cap on his head, and his eyes electrified KC's heart. Since then, she has traveled the world with her prince for almost fifty years as an army family. Today, she is sitting on Sunset Boulevard with her prince as they praise God every day for living the American dream.